CREATIVE
HOMEOWNER®

cabinets & countertops

step by step

CREATIVE HOMEOWNER®, Upper Saddle River, New Jersey

CREATIVE HOMEOWNER®

A Division of Federal Marketing Corp.
Upper Saddle River, NJ

SMART GUIDE: CABINETS & COUNTERTOPS

CONTRIBUTING EDITOR Steve Willson
EDITOR Lisa Kahn
GRAPHIC DESIGNER Kathryn Wityk
PHOTO COORDINATOR Mary Dolan
DIGITAL IMAGING SPECIALIST Frank Dyer
GRAPHIC DESIGN INTERN Larissa Stuts
INDEXER Schroeder Indexing Services
SMART GUIDE® SERIES COVER DESIGN Clark Barre
FRONT COVER PHOTOGRAPHY John Parsekian/CH

CREATIVE HOMEOWNER

VICE PRESIDENT AND PUBLISHER Timothy O. Bakke
MANAGING EDITOR Fran J. Donegan
ART DIRECTOR David Geer
PRODUCTION COORDINATOR Sara M. Markowitz

Current Printing (last digit)
10 9 8 7 6 5 4 3 2 1

Manufactured in the United States of America

Smart Guide: Cabinets & Countertops, First Edition
Library of Congress Control Number: 2010921123
ISBN-10: 1-58011-501-2
ISBN-13: 978-1-58011-501-8

CREATIVE HOMEOWNER®
A Division of Federal Marketing Corp.
24 Park Way
Upper Saddle River, NJ 07458
www.creativehomeowner.com

Planet Friendly Publishing

- ✓ Made in the United States
- ✓ Printed on Recycled Paper
  Text: 10% Cover: 10%

Learn more: www.greenedition.org

At Creative Homeowner we're committed to producing books in an earth-friendly manner and to helping our customers make greener choices.

Manufacturing books in the United States ensures compliance with strict environmental laws and eliminates the need for international freight shipping, a major contributor to global air pollution.

And printing on recycled paper helps minimize our consumption of trees, water, and fossil fuels. *Smart Guide: Cabinets & Countertops* was printed on paper made with 10% post-consumer waste. According to the Environmental Defense Fund Paper Calculator, by using this innovative paper instead of conventional papers we achieved the following environmental benefits:

Trees Saved: 10

Water Saved: 4,808 gallons

Solid Waste Eliminated: 292 pounds

Greenhouse Gas Emissions Eliminated: 998 pounds

For more information on our environmental practices, please visit us online at www.creativehomeowner.com/green

contents

safety first

Though all the designs and methods in this book have been reviewed for safety, it is not possible to overstate the importance of using safe construction methods. What follows are reminders; some do's and don'ts of basic carpentry. They are not substitutes for your own common sense.

- *Always* use caution, care, and good judgment when following the procedures described in this book.
- *Always* be sure that the electrical setup is safe; be sure that no circuit is overloaded and that all power tools and electrical outlets are properly grounded. Do not use power tools in wet locations.
- *Always* read container labels on paints, solvents, and other products; provide ventilation, and observe all other warnings.
- *Always* read the manufacturer's instructions for using a tool, especially the warnings.
- *Always* use hold-downs and push sticks whenever possible when working on a table saw. Avoid working short pieces if you can.
- *Always* remove the key from any drill chuck (portable or press) before starting the drill.
- *Always* pay deliberate attention to how a tool works so that you can avoid being injured.
- *Always* know the limitations of your tools. Do not try to force them to do what they were not designed to do.
- *Always* make sure that any adjustment is locked before proceeding. For example, always check the rip fence on a table saw or the bevel adjustment on a portable saw before starting to work.
- *Always* clamp small pieces firmly to a bench or other work surface when using a power tool on them.
- *Always* wear the appropriate rubber or work gloves when handling chemicals, moving or stacking lumber, or doing heavy construction.
- *Always* wear a disposable face mask when you create dust by sawing or sanding. Use a special filtering respirator when working with toxic substances and solvents.
- *Always* wear eye protection, especially when using power tools or striking metal on metal or concrete; a chip can fly off, for example, when chiseling concrete.
- *Always* be aware that there is seldom enough time for your body's reflexes to save you from injury from a power tool in a dangerous situation; everything happens too fast. Be *alert!*
- *Always* keep your hands away from the business ends of blades, cutters, and bits.
- *Always* hold a circular saw firmly, usually with both hands so that you know where they are.
- *Always* use a drill with an auxiliary handle to control the torque when large-size bits are used.
- *Always* check your local building codes when planning new construction. The codes are intended to protect public safety and should be observed to the letter.
- *Never* work with power tools when you are tired or under the influence of alcohol or drugs.
- *Never* cut tiny pieces of wood or pipe using a power saw. Cut small pieces off larger pieces.
- *Never* change a saw blade or a drill or router bit unless the power cord is unplugged. Do not depend on the switch being off; you might accidentally hit it.
- *Never* work in insufficient lighting.
- *Never* work while wearing loose clothing, hanging hair, open cuffs, or jewelry.
- *Never* work with dull tools. Have them sharpened, or learn how to sharpen them yourself.
- *Never* use a power tool on a workpiece—large or small—that is not firmly supported.
- *Never* saw a workpiece that spans a large distance between horses without close support on each side of the cut; the piece can bend, closing on and jamming the blade, causing saw kickback.
- *Never* support a workpiece from underneath with your leg or other part of your body when sawing.
- *Never* carry sharp or pointed tools, such as utility knives, awls, or chisels, in your pocket. If you want to carry such tools, use a special-purpose tool belt with leather pockets and holders.

introduction

Cabinets and countertops form the backbone of every kitchen. From breakfast cereals to cake mixers to frying pans, cabinets hold all the tools and supplies you need. And the countertops attached to them are the surfaces where just about all the work gets done. Generally, the more of both you have, the happier you are with your kitchen. To a lesser degree, the same is true of your bathroom. The bigger the vanity, the more storage room it has, and the more counter area it provides for toothpaste, shaving gear, and hair dryers. But kitchens and bathrooms are the not only rooms that contain cabinetry. Just about every room in the house can benefit from more storage and workspace. Laundry rooms, basements, garages, walk-in closets, large linen closets, and even attics boast at least a cabinet or two, especially in newer houses.

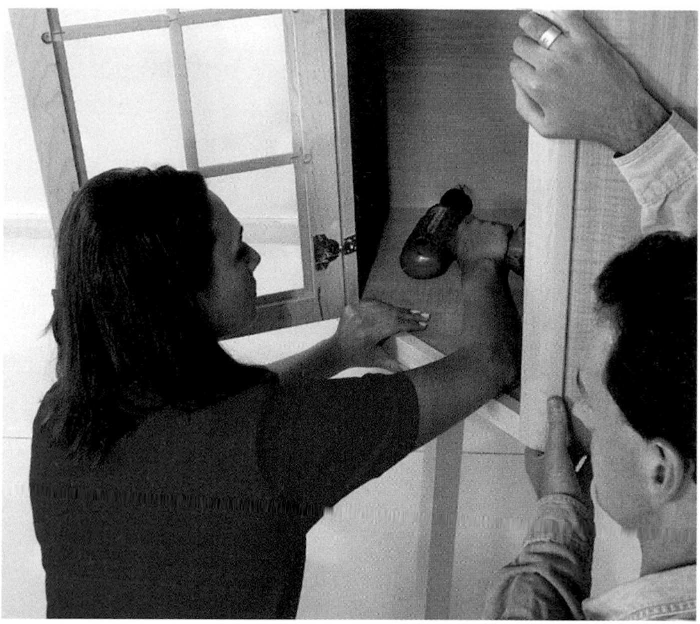

If you have some basic carpentry skills, you can install your own cabinets like a pro.

Today's cabinetry choices are a marvel of high-tech design and functionality.

Buying Cabinets. You have almost as many ways to buy cabinets as you have places to put them. If you are remodeling a kitchen or bathroom, it pays to visit a cabinet showroom. The salespeople usually know a lot about cabinets and room design. Larger stores and most home centers may even have a designer to help you make the most out of your room. This service is often free if you buy your cabinets from the store. But even if you have to pay, consider it money well spent. If you already know what cabinets you want and you are confident about your room design, then you can shop at lumberyards and home retailers. The selection (and the quality) won't be as broad as a cabinet store's, but the prices can be quite a bit less.

Building Cabinets. If you are ambitious and have some cabinetmaking experience, you can build your own cabinets and countertops as is shown later in this book. This approach can yield wonderful results for less money than you'll spend on high-quality manufactured cabinets. And you can size everything to accommodate your design instead of making your plans fit stock cabinet sizes.

For the very best results, consider custom-made cabinetry. If you hire somebody who has a good reputation, you will receive furniture-quality craftsmanship. Of course, this route is the most expensive and would be hard to justify for a garage cabinet job. But for your kitchen, bathrooms, and closets it can add a lot of value to your house.

Finding a design and a price that you like, however, are not the only considerations. Also keep in mind how the cabinets function. Over the last 20 years, many types of clever cabinet hardware have become available for professionals and homeowners alike. Using this hardware makes a standard cabinet with a single door pretty passé. Sliding shelves, rotating shelves, pot-lid racks, spice drawers, and much, much more can make just about any base or wall cabinet into a marvel of convenience and high design.

chapter 1

tools

Getting Started

Many people new to do-it-yourself projects are surprised to learn how much they can accomplish with a few hand and power tools. It doesn't take a shop full of expensive machinery to install kitchen or bathroom cabinets or to add a new countertop—although if you are going to install ceramic tile on a countertop, you will need some speciality tools. And if you are planning to tackle the building projects in Chapter 7, you will need more-advanced tools.

Here's a list of hand tools you'll need for installing cabinets and countertops. Below this list, you'll find a descriptions of tools that aren't essential but will help you work more efficiently, especially if build your own cabinets.

Hammers. For cabinet and countertop installation, you will need a standard claw hammer for driving and removing nails.

Steel Tape Measure. Tape measures commonly come in lengths from 6 to 50 feet. A 16-footer will serve fine for any project in this book. If you want to use the tape measure for carpentry work as well, choose a 25-footer. Good quality tapes have ¾-inch-wide blades that can stay rigid up to about 7 feet.

Levels. To determine whether cabinets are installed level and plumb, use a level. Levels are made of wood, metal, or plastic. New electronic digital levels are also capable of checking other angles. Levels come in lengths from 9 inches to more than 72 inches. Choose 4- and 2-foot levels. The longer level will provde accurate readings on cabinets. The 2-foot level is small enough for working in tight quarters yet long enough to provide an accurate reading.

Utility Knife. Always make sure the blade is sharp because dull blades aren't as precise and may slip off the cutting line as you pull the knife to cut.

Screwdrivers. Although they may rank as one of the simplest tools found in any toolbox, a good set of screwdrivers is essential for the do-it-yourselfer. The two most common types of screwdrivers are the flat-blade and the Phillips head. The best way to avoid stripping screwheads is to have a good selection of different-size screwdrivers to properly fit the different size screws.

For large projects, drive screws using a drill/driver outfitted with a screwdriver attachment.

Basic Cabinet Installation Tools

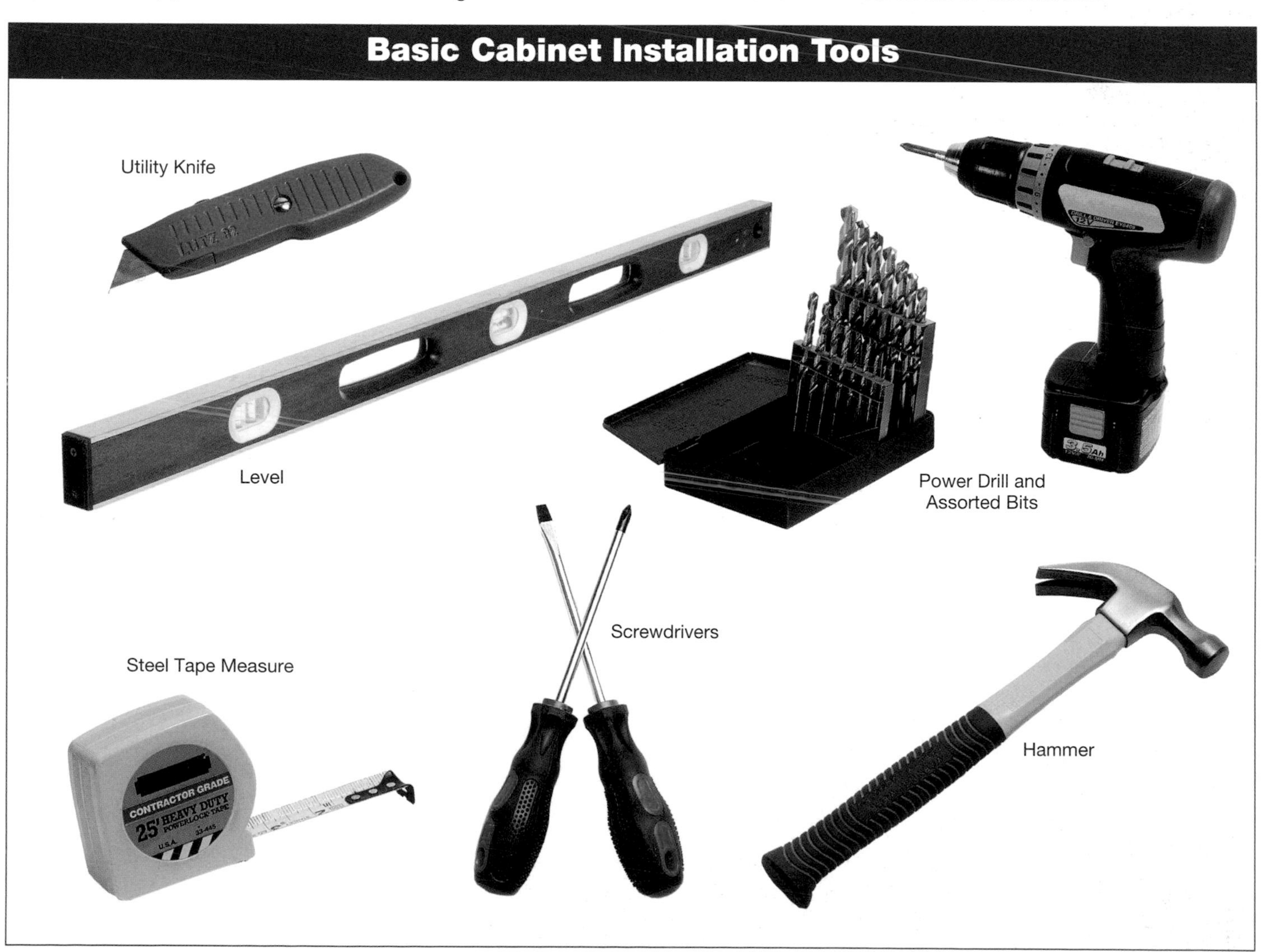

Measuring Tools and Squares

Measuring Tools

Folding Rule. Sometimes a tape measure just won't do—as in measuring in tight spots—or isn't accurate enough. In these cases a traditional folding wooden rule is the answer.

Squares

Squares are tools that are invaluable for measuring, marking, and checking the inside and outside squareness of right angles.

Framing Square. Available in a few sizes, the traditional framing square has a 24-inch-long blade and 16-inch-long tongue and is the tool of choice for house framing work. You may find one of the smaller models, measuring 8 x 6 or 12 x 8 inches, more convenient for smaller projects.

Try Square. The blade of the try square, which may be graduated for measurement, is available in lengths from 2 to 12 inches. This blade is attached to an unmarked block of hardwood or plastic. Use a try square to test, or try, the squareness of right angles, to scribe lines, and to calibrate tools. One type, called a try-and-miter square has a 45-degree surface in the block so that it can scribe miters.

Combination Square. Consisting of a 6-, 12-, or 16-inch graduated steel blade, the combination square has a sliding handle that can be tightened at any position. Most come equipped with a spirit level and scratch awl built into the handle. This square is one of the most useful tools in any woodworker's shop. You can use it to check for level or plumb or make 90- or 45-degree angles. It serves as a try sqaure, depth gauge, marking gauge, and straightedge. It's also the ideal tool for locating and centering screw holes and scribing layout lines.

Sliding Adjustable Bevel Gauge. A bevel gauge consists of a handle or stock attached to a 6- or 8-inch slotted blade. It is commonly used in the workshop for duplicating angles other than 90 degrees. Set the tool, and transfer exact angles from place to place.

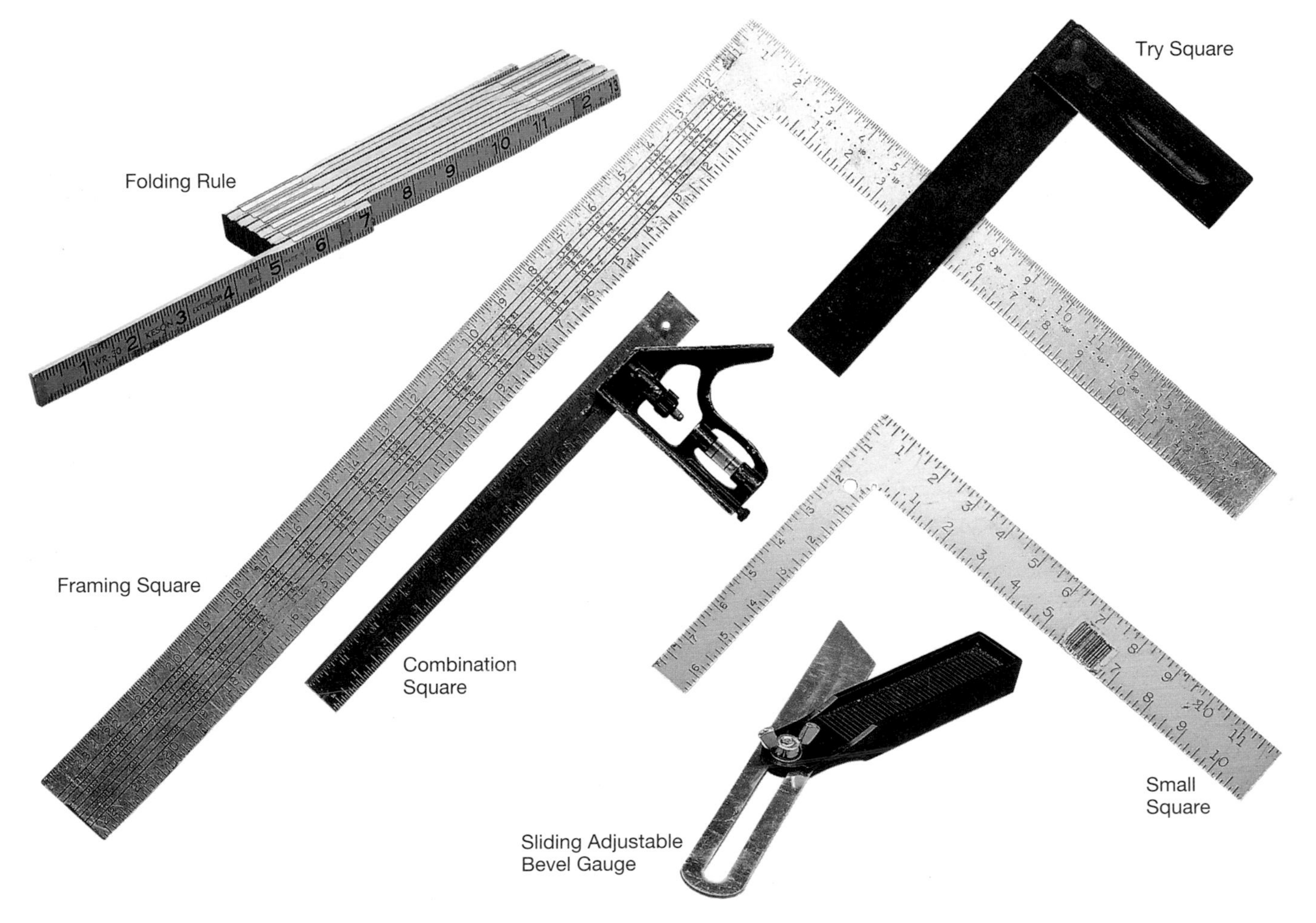

Safety Equipment

Common sense should tell you not to attempt any project without adequate eye and ear protection. Wear safety goggles or plastic glasses whenever you are working with tools or chemicals, period. Make sure that your eye protection conforms to those requirements set by either the American National Standards Institute (ANSI) or Canadian Standards Association (CSA).

The U.S. Occupational Safety and Health Administration (OSHA) recommends that hearing protection be worn whenever the noise level exceeds 85 decibels (dB) for an 8-hour workday. Considering that a circular saw emits 110 dB, even shorter exposure times are dangerous. Insert and muff-type protectors are available; make sure that you choose models with a noise reduction rating (NNR) of at least 20 dB. Because sawdust is a by-product of any project, it's a good idea to wear a dust mask. Two types of masks are available: disposable dust masks and cartridge-type respirators. A dust mask is good for protecting you from most fine particles. Respirators generally offer superior protection but also have certain disadvantages. With a respirator, breathing is more labored, and it can get warm inside the mask. Whichever you purchase, be sure that it has been stamped by the National Institute for Occupational Safety & Health/Mine Safety and Health Administration (NIOSH/MSHA) and is approved for your specific operation. If you can taste or smell the contaminate or if the mask starts to interfere with normal breathing, it's time for a replacement.

Safety Equipment: (A) rubber gloves, (B) ear protectors, (C) hard hat, (D) knee pads, (E) work gloves, (F) filtered respirator, (G) safety glasses, (H) safety goggles, (I) ear plugs, (J) particle mask

Other Helpful Hand Tools

You'll need some other tools to help with the projects, especially the building projects found in Chapter 7.

Nail Sets and Center Punches. A nail set is used to drive finishing nails below the work surface without denting the surface, so the holes can be easily filled. A set rests on top of a nail or brad, enabling you to safely sink the nail without damaging the surrounding wood. The standard three-piece set—consisting of 1/32-, 1/16-, and 3/32-inch nail sets—will handle most of the jobs for the home workshop.

A center punch looks like a nail set, except that its sharp, conical point tends to stick into wood. You'll need one for locating and punching starter holes for twist-drill bits to keep them from "walking" off their mark during the initial drilling. Starter holes are also handy when hand-driving screws.

Nail sets

Wood Chisels

Designed for removing wood in chips, chunks, and shavings, wood chisels can be driven with a mallet or manipulated by hand for precise paring. They are particularly handy for making quick work of hinge mortises. A four-chisel set including 1/4-, 1/2-, 3/4-, and 1-inch chisels should cover most needs in the home workshop.

Chisels

An old shop rule warns against striking a chisel with anything but a wooden or leather mallet. This rule still holds with wooden chisels; the blade tangs can split the handle if the tool is used improperly. Modern plastic-handled chisels, however, are much more durable and can be used with ordinary steel hammers.

Planes

Although they're not essential for the projects in this book, few tools can remove paper-thin wood shavings or smooth a rough board as efficiently as a hand plane. Basic planes include the block plane, smooth plane, and jack plane.

The block plane is designed for trimming end grain. It can also be useful for easing the backs of mitered joints or planing down edging flush with a plywood panel.

Jack planes and smooth planes are types of bench plane. They look very similar to each other, with both having blades about 1 3/4 to 2 inches wide, but they differ in length. Jack planes are between 6 and 10 inches long. Smooth planes range from 11 to 14 inches long.

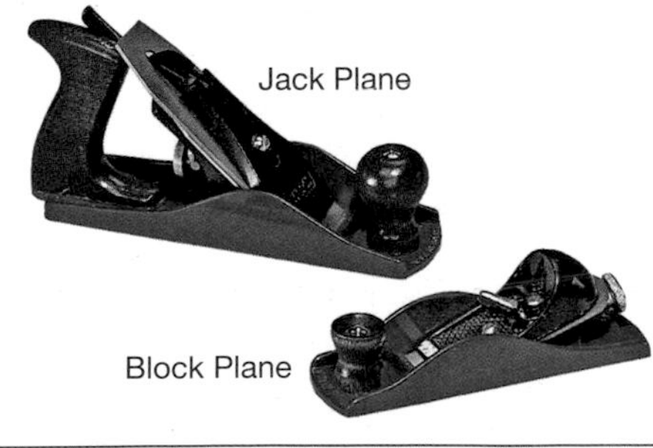
Jack Plane

Block Plane

Saws

You'll need a handsaw for cutting wood and wood products and a hacksaw for cutting metal. For some decorative curves, you may find a need for a coping saw. For other chores, you might want to buy a backsaw or special dovetail and veneer saws.

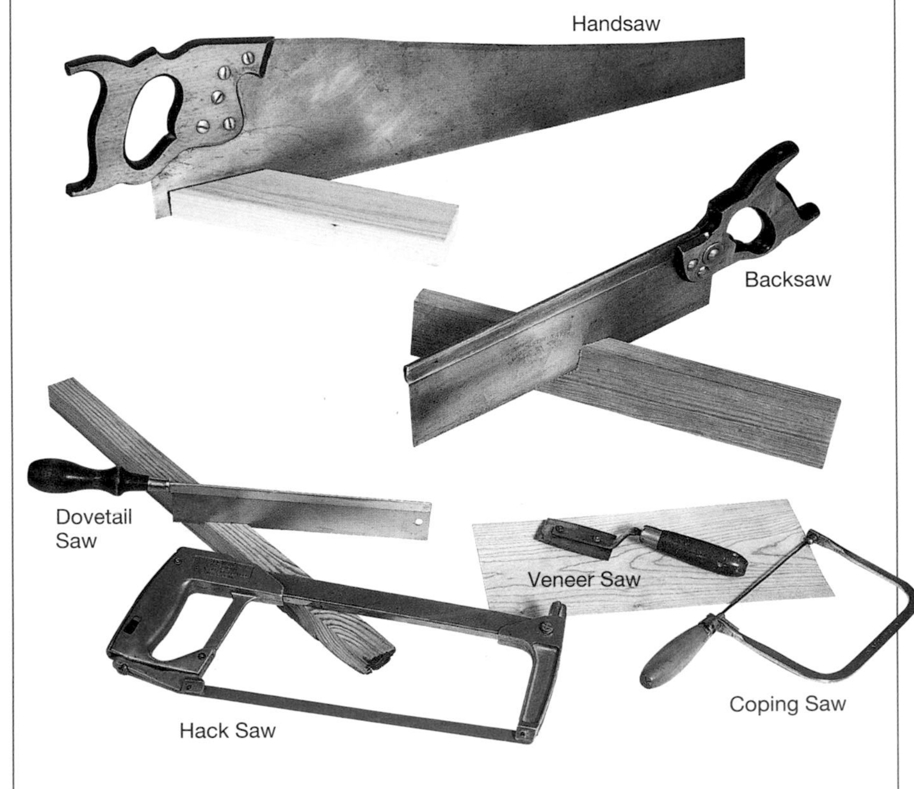
Handsaw

Backsaw

Dovetail Saw

Veneer Saw

Hack Saw

Coping Saw

Clamps and Vises

No shop ever has enough clamps, vises, or handscrews, yet these essential tools are most often overlooked by beginning do-it-yourselfers. Clamps are designed for such jobs as edge-gluing boards and attaching trim to plywood edges. It won't take long for you to discover how valuable they can be throughout your shop. Use clamps to secure workpieces for sawing, routing, drilling, or sanding. A good basic starter set consists of a pair or two of 4-inch C-clamps, at least one pair of pipe clamps, and some spring clamps.

Bar Clamps and Pipe Clamps. Bar clamps provide greater reach than most other clamps and are ideal for drawing frame members and cabinet panels together. They range in size from about 1 to 8 feet. Bar clamps of 24 to 36 inches will see to many chores in the home workshop and aren't prohibitively expensive. Big bar clamps, however, might prove too costly for the do-it-yourselfer on a tight budget.

Pipe clamps offer a less-expensive alternative, especially for big clamping tasks. These clamps, consisting of cast-iron fixtures that you thread onto lengths of separately purchased black-iron pipe, are available from home centers, hardware stores, and mail-order sources. You should be able to buy threaded pipe at a home center, otherwise you may have to go to a store that specializes in plumbing supplies. A pair of 48-inch pipe clamps will take care of most jobs. When you need something bigger, you can simply join two pieces of pipe with a pipe coupler.

Strap Clamps. Consisting of a fabric strap that fits around the work, the strap clamp has hardware that lets you tighten the tension on the strap as if you were tightening a seat belt. Strap clamps work best on unusually shaped surfaces.

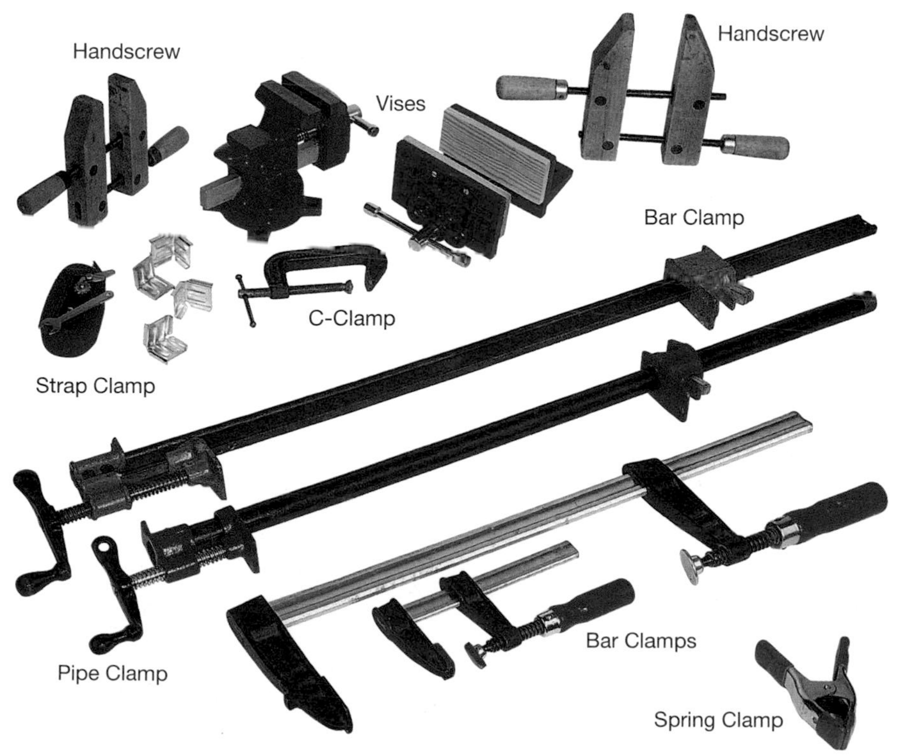

Power Tools

To build cabinets, you'll need an electric drill, saber saw, circular saw, router, and electric sander. You can get by without any stationary power tools, but a bench-top table saw can save a lot of time when you need to cut sheet stock, mill grooves or rabbets, and tackle a great variety of other sawing chores.

Drills, Bits & Accessories

Look for a ⅜-inch, variable-speed, reversible drill for everyday use. Cordless drills may be more expensive, but they are the most convenient. Today there are 12-volt cordless drill/drivers powerful enough to handle most tasks. Many come with keyless chucks, adjustable clutches, and driver-bit storage. If you decide to purchase one, consider buying an extra battery as a backup power supply.

Basic Bits. Invest in a set of twist-drill or brad-point bits with sizes from 1⁄16 to ¼ inch; you can always buy the larger sizes as you need them. Brad-point bits cost a little more but are better for drilling wood. Their pointed tips are less apt to skid across your work, and they generally bore cleaner holes. For most larger wood-boring chores, you can get by with inexpensive spade bits for holes up to 1½ inches in diameter and hole saws for boring holes up to 2½ inches in diameter. You'll also want screwdriver bits, which you can buy individually or in sets for standard slotted, Phillips, and other types of screws.

Countersink and Counterbore Bits. Invest in a set of inexpensive countersink bits for drilling and countersinking holes for screws in sizes from #4 to #12. Although you can drill, countersink, and counterbore screw holes with ordinary drill bits, counterboring bits can perform all three functions in one step.

Doweling Jig. For assembling furniture and cabinets with dowels, you'll need a doweling jig. It will enable you to drill perfectly aligned holes.

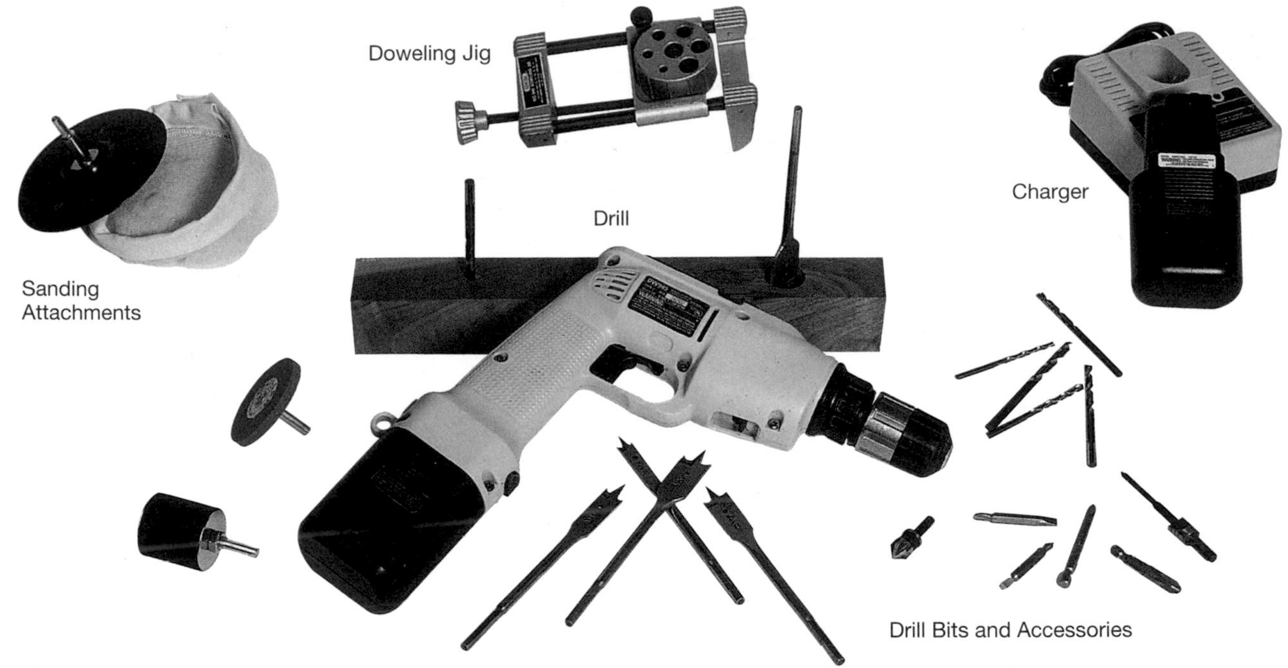

Portable Power Saws

Saber Saw. Use a saber saw with a saw guide to cut straight lines or freehand to make pocket cuts, circular cuts, and other cuts of unusual shape. A saber saw is excellent for cutting and trimming panel stock, back-cutting large moldings, and making cutouts in countertops. With the right blade you can use a saber saw to cut metal, plastic pipe, laminates, or Plexiglas. Look for a saw that has orbital action (which advances the blade on the cutting stroke), for faster cutting speeds and longer-lasting blades.

Circular Saw. A workhorse that is as indispensable in the home workshop as it is on a commercial construction site, the standard circular saw uses a 7¼-inch blade that can crosscut or rip stock up to 2½ inches thick, which means this saw will easily handle nominal 1-inch and 2-inch lumber and all sheet stock.

There are various blades available for the circular saw designed for crosscutting, ripping, and other specific chores and materials, as well as general-purpose combination blades that will do several jobs fairly well. Generally, the more teeth a blade has, the finer it will cut; a 7¼-inch circular blade with 36 to 40 carbide-tipped teeth will provide a reasonably splinter-free cut.

Circular Saw and Router Guides. Without any kind of guide, a circular saw can make cuts that are straight enough for carpentry work. However, to make cuts straight and square enough for cabinet work, you'll need a guide. Router bits designed to shape edges have their own pilots, but a guide is essential to mill dadoes and grooves with the router.

You can buy a guide that attaches to a circular saw and runs along the edge of the board as you make a cut. This kind of guide works only for cuts that are within a few inches of the edge. As a result, it is useful mainly for making rip cuts along the length of a board or panel. This can be handy if you don't have a table saw for ripping. You can buy a similar sort of guide to attach to your router, but you won't need one for the projects in this book.

A more versatile approach to guiding both the circular saw and the router is to use a purchased prefabricated metal straightedge guide that you clamp to the work. You can also buy guides that have clamps built in.

Saber Saw

Circular Saw

Routers, Bits, and Accessories

The router ranks just behind drills and saws in popularity among woodworkers. This versatile tool deserves its place in the workshop because of its capacity to perform a tremendous variety of tasks, such as making rabbets, dadoes, and grooves; routing decorative edges in wood; making moldings; and cutting plastic laminates.

All routers are basically a motor with a straight-shaft cutter mounted on a base. The wide range in prices largely reflects differences in power: ⅓- to ½-horsepower (hp) models are considered light-duty, while heavy-duty models are powered by 2- to 3-hp motors. Also, some routers can plunge the bit into the work, a feature you won't need for the projects in this book. If you are purchasing one router for general purposes, get one with about 1½ horsepower.

Basic Bits. Outfit your router with a set of basic bits, including straight, roundover, rabbeting, cove, and chamfering bits. If you plan to laminate your countertops, you'll also need a flush-trimming bit. All of these bits, except the straight bit, are piloted edge-shaping bits. Some bits are piloted by a ball-bearing guide that runs along the edge of the wood. Bits are also available with fixed pilots that spin with the bit. These are cheaper, but the friction of the spinning pilot often burns the edge of the wood.

Router Table. You can buy or build a router table. This accessory lets your router function like a small shaper. A table is ideal for many applications where it's easier or safer to bring the material to the tool, instead of vice versa. This is the preferred way to make your own moldings and to mill decorative edges on panels, such as drawer fronts.

Router

Plunge Router

Sanders

No chore is as tedious as hand sanding. A general-duty electric sander will save untold amounts of time and will help produce a more uniform finish.

Pad Sander. Also known as finishing sanders, pad sanders are available in three popular sizes to accommodate ¼, ⅓, or ½ sheets of sandpaper. The ⅓-sheet and ½-sheet sanders are designed for two-handed operation, while the ¼-sheet models, often called palm sanders, are for one-handed use. Pad sanders sand in an orbital motion for fast material removal or straight-line motion for fine finishing; some can be switched between the two modes.

Random-Orbit Disc Sander. This sander is popular with woodworkers because it removes wood faster than a pad sander while its random orbit eliminates the swirls you get with a pad sander.

Pad Sanders

Random-Orbit Sanders

chapter 2

cabinet design

The Basic Cabinet

Cabinets come in many different styles and are constructed of a wide range of materials—from medium-density fiberboard at the low end up to solid walnut or cherry at the high end. But no matter what their style and materials, most cabinets come in only three basic designs. The first, and most common, is the basic box with a single door. These are used for base cabinets and wall cabinets alike and handle the bulk of the storage in the kitchen, bath, or utility room. The second type is the cabinet that is filled with drawers from bottom to top. These cabinets usually hold four relatively shallow drawers that are designed to store small, loose items such as cooking utensils and personal-care products. The last type is a combination of the first two. It features a top-mounted drawer above a single cabinet door. The drawer supplies small parts storage while the cabinet holds larger items. Of course, this is a simplified view of cabinet design. These three-basic designs are the basis for the wide variety of cabinet styles found in any home. Cabinet variations include glass doors, double-wide cabinets, and storage options.

Choose from a variety of possible cabinet finishes. Choices range from natural looks, right, to glazed and painted finishes, below.

Framed cabinets—those with a full frame across the cabinet box—are often used in traditional kitchens.

Cabinet Styles and Options

While it's true that cabinets help define the style and create the environment of a kitchen, their main job is to store the many items involved in preparing, serving, and cleaning up after meals. They must be durable enough to withstand thousands of openings and closings over years of use.

Regardless of the type and style of cabinets you choose, insist on quality construction. Good cabinets feature dovetail and mortise-and-tenon joinery and solidly mortised hinges. The interiors are well finished, with adjustable shelves that are a minimum of ⅝ inch thick to prevent bowing under heavy loads. The drawers in good cabinets roll on ball-bearing glides, and they support at least 75 pounds when open.

Construction Styles and Options

There are basically two construction styles for kitchen cabinetry: framed and frameless. You can buy inexpensive ready-made cabinets directly from a retailer's stock in finished form, in unfinished form, or as knockdowns. These will usually be framed cabinets. If you prefer, choose more expensive semi-custom and custom-made cabinets. You can get custom cabinets from a large manufacturer, or have them built to your room's specifications by a carpenter or cabinetmaker.

Framed. Framed cabinets—or traditional-style cabinets—have a full frame across the face of the cabinet box. This provides a means of securing adjacent cabinets together and strengthens wider cabinet boxes with a center rail. Hinges may be either visible or hidden, and the front frame may or may not be visible around doors and drawers when they are closed.

Frameless. Frameless cabinets—also known as European-style cabinets—are built without a face frame. Close-fitting doors cover the entire front of the box, or they may be set into the box opening. Hinges are typically hidden. Both domestic and European manufacturers offer frameless cabinets. Prices can be high and delivery times lengthy if you want features that an import dealer does not have in stock.

Manufacturing Styles

Unless you have the time and skill to build the cabinets yourself, or you can hire someone else to do it, you'll have to purchase them in one of three ways: stock, semi-custom, or custom. Prices vary from category to category, and even within each category.

Stock. Stock cabinets are literally in stock where they are sold or are quickly available by order. They are made in limited styles and colors but in a wide variety of standard sizes that you can assemble to suit your kitchen space. The quality of stock cabinets may be fair, good, or excellent, depending on the manufacturer and price. Materials may be solid wood (hard or soft) and plywood, wood and particleboard, wood and hardboard, or all particleboard. They may be carefully jointed and doweled or merely nailed and glued together. Stock cabinets also come in steel and in several types of plastic, either in part or entirely. The quality of cabinets made from these materials also varies from barely adequate to exquisite. Stock cabinets range in price from inexpensive models to moderately costly units.

You can save some money by buying unfinished stock cabinets and staining or painting them yourself. You can save even more by purchasing knockdown cabinets, which are shipped flat to lower the costs of packing and delivery. You assemble the cabinets yourself on site. Knockdowns are sometimes unfinished as well.

Semi-Custom. Like stock cabinets, semi-custom cabinets are available only in specific sizes, but there are many more finishes, colors, styles, options, and special features to chose from than you will find with stock cabinets. The extras aren't added to the cabinets until you place the order, so there will be a wait for delivery. Times vary, but expect to wait three to six weeks for delivery.

Custom. Custom cabinets are built to the measurements of a particular project. Because custom cabinets are made from scratch, delivery may take from 4 to 16 weeks. The delivery delay rarely causes a problem because the preparation work for a new kitchen also takes time. But place your order well in advance of the date you will need your cabinets. Custom cabinets are almost always delivered completely finished, like fine furniture, whereas some stock cabinets may be bought unfinished. Prices for custom cabinets run from moderate to very expensive.

Carpenter-Built. If you have the time, some carpentry skills, and a work area, you can save money by constructing cabinets to your own specifications. Keep in mind that this work can be very time-consuming. Or you can hire a carpenter to build them. This won't be a money saver, of course, but will give you great leeway in your design.

Semi-custom cabinets are available with a variety of options, including matching refrigerator panels.

Spice drawers and open shelves are popular design elements.

Storage Options

The type of storage in a kitchen is almost as important as the amount. Some people like at least a few open shelves for displaying attractive china or glassware; others want absolutely everything tucked away behind doors.

What are your storage needs? The answer depends partly on your food shopping habits and partly on how many pots, pans, and other pieces of kitchen equipment you have or would like to have. A family that goes food shopping several times a week and prepares mostly fresh foods needs more refrigerator space, less freezer capacity, and fewer cabinets than a family that prefers packaged or prepared foods and makes only infrequent forays to the local supermarket.

Planning

To help clarify your needs, mentally walk yourself through a typical meal and list the utensils used to prepare food, where you got them, and your progress throughout the work area. And don't limit yourself to full-scale meals. Much kitchen work is devoted to preparing snacks, reheating leftovers, and making lunches for the kids to take to school.

Food Preparation. During food preparation, the sink and stove come into use. Some families rely heavily on the microwave for reheating. Using water means repeated trips to the sink, so that area might be the best place to keep a steamer, salad spinner, and coffee and tea canisters, as well as glassware and cups. Near the stove you may want storage for odd-shaped items such as a fish poacher or wok. You can hang frequently used pans and utensils from a convenient rack; stow other items in cabinets so that they do not collect grease.

During the Meal. When the food is ready, you must take it to the table. If the eating space is nearby, a work counter might turn into a serving counter. If the dining space is in another room, a pass-through facilitates serving.

After the Meal. When the meal ends, dishes must go from the table to the sink or dishwasher, and leftovers to storage containers and the refrigerator. Now the stove and counters need to be wiped down and the sink scoured. When the dishwasher finishes its cycle, everything must be put away.

Order cabinets that suit your storage needs. Mentally walk through a typical day in the kitchen to find what works best.

Storage Checklist

- **Do you like kitchen gadgets?** Plan drawer space, countertop sorters, wall magnets, or hooks to keep these items handy near where you often use them.
- **Do you own a food processor, blender, mixer, toaster oven, knife sharpener, juicer, coffee maker, or coffee mill?** If you're particularly tidy, you may want small appliances like these tucked away in an appliance garage or cupboard to be taken out only when needed. If you prefer to have frequently used machines sitting on the counter, ready to go, plan enough space, along with conveniently located electrical outlets.
- **Do you plan to store large quantities of food?** Be sure to allow plenty of freezer, bin, and shelf space for the kind of food shopping you do.
- **Do you intend to do a lot of freezing or canning?** Allow a work space and place to stow equipment. Also plan adequate freezer storage.
- **Do you bake often?** Consider a baking center that can house your equipment and serve as a separate baking pantry.
- **Do you collect pottery, tinware, or anything else that might be displayed in the kitchen?** Eliminating soffits provides a shelf on top of the wall cabinets for collectibles.
- **Do you collect cookbooks?** If so, you'll need expandable shelf space and perhaps a bookstand.

Personal Profile of You and Your Family

- **How tall are you and everyone else who will use your kitchen?** Adjust your counter and wall-cabinet heights to suit.
- **Do you or any of your family members use a walker, leg braces, or a wheelchair?** Plan a good work height, knee space, grab bars, secure seating, slide-out work boards, and other convenience features.
- **Are you left- or right-handed?** Think about your natural motion when you choose whether to open cupboards or refrigerator doors from the left or right.
- **How high can you comfortably reach?** If you're tall, hang your wall cabinets high. If you're petite, you may want to hang the cabinets lower and plan a spot to keep a step-stool handy.
- **Can you comfortably bend and reach for something in a base cabinet?** Can you lift heavy objects easily and without strain or pain? If your range is limited in these areas, be sure to plan roll-out shelving on both upper and lower tiers of your base cabinets. Also, look into spring-up shelves designed to lift mixer bases or other heavy appliances to counter height.
- **Do you frequently share cooking tasks with another family member?** If so, you may each prefer to have your own work area.

Types of Storage

Storage facilities can make or break a kitchen, so choose the places you'll put things with care. Here's a look at a few alternatives:

Open versus Closed Storage. Shelves, pegboards, pot racks, cup hooks, magnetic knife racks, and the like put your utensils on view, which is a good way to personalize your kitchen. Here's an area where you can save some money, too. Open storage generally costs less than cabinets, and you don't have to construct and hang doors.

But open storage has drawbacks. For one thing, items left out in the open can look messy unless they are kept neatly arranged. Also, objects collect dust and grease, especially near the range. This means that unless you reach for an item almost daily, you'll find yourself washing it before as well as after you use it.

Closed storage like under-counter pantries, above, keep items close to their point of use. Glass-fronted cabinets, below, put your favorite items on display.

If extra washing and dusting discourages you from the idea of open storage but you'd like to put at least some objects on view, limit your displays to a few items. Another option is to install glass doors on wall cabinets. This handily solves the dust problem but often costs more than solid doors.

Pantries. How often you shop and how many groceries you typically bring home determine the amount of food storage space your family needs. If you like to stock up or take advantage of sales, add a pantry to your kitchen. To maximize a pantry's convenience, plan shallow, 6-inch-deep shelves so that cans and packages will never be stored more than two deep. This way, you'll easily be able to see what you've got on hand. Pantries range in size from floor-to-ceiling models to narrow units designed to fit between two standard-size cabinets.

Specialty storage is key to a well-designed kitchen. A full-height pantry can hold supplies for the long term.

Appliance Garages. Appliance garages make use of dead space in a corner, but they can be installed anywhere in the vertical space between wall-mounted cabinets and the countertop. A tambour (rolltop) door hides small appliances like a food processor or anything else you want within reach but hidden from view. This form of minicabinet can be equipped with an electrical outlet and even can be divided into separate sections to store more than one item. Customize an appliance garage any way you like. Reserve part of the appliance garage for cookbook storage, for example, or outfit it with small drawers for little items or spices.

Appliance garages keep countertop appliances in easy reach but out of sight when not in use.

A revolving shelf placed near the cooking center is a good place to store spices.

(continued on next page)

Types of Storage (continued)

Lazy Susans and Carousel Shelves. Rotating shelves like lazy Susans and carousels maximize dead corner storage and put items such as dishes, or pots and pans, within easy reach. A lazy Susan rotates 360 degrees, so just spin it to find what you're looking for. Carousel shelves, which attach to two right-angled doors, rotate 270 degrees; open the doors, and the shelves swing out allowing you to reach items easily. Pivoting shelves are a variation on the carousel design and may or may not be door mounted. In addition, units may be built into taller cabinets, creating a pantry that can store a lot in a small amount of space.

Fold-Down Mixer Shelf. A spring-loaded mixer shelf swings up and out of a base cabinet for use, then folds down and back into the cabinet when the mixer is no longer needed.

Slide-Outs and Tilt-Outs. Installed in base cabinets, slide-out trays and racks store small appliances, linens, cans, or boxed items, while slide-out bins are good for holding onions, potatoes, grains, pet food, or potting soil—even garbage or recycling containers. A tilt-out tray is located in the often-wasted area just below the lip of the countertop in front of the sink and above base cabinet doors. Use it to hold sponges and cloths.

Pivoting Shelves. Door-mounted shelves and in-cabinet swiveling shelf units offer easy access to kitchen supplies. Taller units serve as pantries that hold a great deal in minimal space.

Pullout Tables and Trays. In tight kitchens, pullout tables and trays are excellent ways to gain eating space or an extra work surface. Pullout cutting boards come in handy near cooktops and microwaves. Pullout tea carts are also available.

Drawer Inserts. A drawer insert is a good way to keep packaged spices organized and easily accessible. Inserts are made for flatware and other items, too.

Tray Storage. A narrow base cabinet with horizontal slots is perfect for storing cookie sheets and trays on edge.

Pivoting shelves save you from stooping to retrieve items from the back of base cabinets.

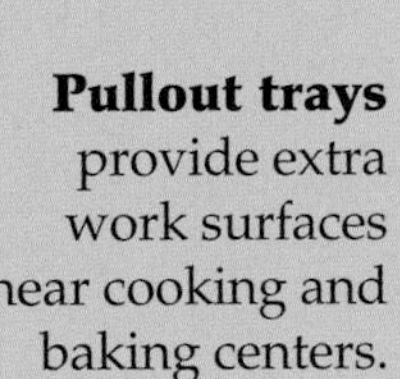

Pullout trays provide extra work surfaces near cooking and baking centers.

Turn wasted space to valuable storage with pull-out tray holders.

Customized Organizers. If you decide to make do with your existing cabinets, consider refitting their interiors with cabinet organizers. These plastic, plastic-coated wire, or enameled-steel racks and hangers are widely available at department stores, hardware stores, and home centers. And they cover just about every type of specialized storage you can imagine. Some of these units slide in and out of base cabinets, similar to the racks in a dishwasher. Others let you mount shallow drawers to the undersides of wall cabinets. Still others consist of stackable plastic bins with plenty of room to hold kitchen sundries.

Beware of the temptation to overspecialize your kitchen storage facilities. Sizes and needs for certain items change, so be sure to allot at least 50 percent of your kitchen's storage to standard cabinets with one or more movable shelves.

Recycling Storage. Slide-out shelves can hold two or three large containers for sorting recyclable materials. Some products also include bins for holding newspapers.

Herb and Spice Racks. Be aware that herbs and spices lose their flavor more rapidly when exposed to heat or sunlight, so don't locate a spice rack or shelving intended for storing herbs too close to the cooktop or a sunny window. Choose opaque containers, or keep seasonings in a cool, closed cupboard or in a drawer outfitted with a rack so you can quickly reach what you need.

Wine Storage. Some contemporary kitchens show off bottles of wine in open racks and bins that hold as much as a couple of cases. If you regularly serve wine with meals, by all means keep a few bottles on hand—but bear in mind that the kitchen is far from the ideal place to store wine for any length of time.

The problem is that heat and sunlight are two of wine's worst enemies, which is why fine wines are stored in cellars. The temperature in a wine cellar should be about 55 to 60 degrees F, so if you'd like to age new vintages for a year or two, keep them in a cool, dark location, such as the basement or an attached climate-controlled garage, where the bottles won't be disturbed.

Glass-front drawers put pasta, beans, or rice on display, making them part of the kitchen's design.

Cabinet Hardware

Door and drawer pulls and knobs not only serve a functional purpose, they also contribute to the overall look of your kitchen. When selecting hardware, make sure you can grip it easily and comfortably. If your fingers or hands get stiff easily or if you have arthritis, select C- or U-shaped pulls because they are easier to grab and hold on to. If you like a knob, try it out in the showroom to make sure it isn't slippery or awkward when you grab it. Knobs and pulls can be inexpensive if you stick to unfinished ones that you can paint in an accent color picked up from the tile or wallpaper. If you don't plan to buy new cabinets, changing the hardware on old ones can redefine their style. The right knob or pull can suggest any one of a number of vintage looks or decorative styles.

Rediscovering the Garage

For years, most homeowners have used their garages for parking cars and storing stuff that doesn't fit anywhere else or is overflow from other parts of the house. The problem is that most garage storage is disorganized—a place where stored items go never to be heard from again.

Rather than using your garage as a storage heap, consider making the space more functional. Many people are remodeling their garages, or one of their garages, to include more living and storage space.

If you like working on cars, why not create a state-of-the-art car-restoration studio? Maybe you'd prefer a furniture-making shop that will be the envy of every craftsman in town, or a big home gym. The point is you will need a storage system to make your plans work.

Part of what's driving this change is the availability of new storage products designed specifically for the garage. And simple common sense also plays a role. Most two-car garages occupy about 500 square feet of space, and that's space that already has a foundation under it, a floor in it, walls around it, and a roof over it. That is 500 square feet of ready-to-use space that you can make into anything you want, including an extra storage area.

It doesn't take long to fill up your garage. One thing leads to another, and before you know it, the cars are out on the driveway, the door is always closed, and there's a note on the refrigerator that says CLEAN OUT THE GARAGE.

A total garage makeover costs some money, especially if you choose high-end cabinets and flooring. But the results look great, create accessible storage for all the essentials, and even leave room for the cars, at least for the time being.

Modular storage systems that include both cabinets and wall-hung options can accommodate just about everything that most people need to store.

Storage Systems

If you want to make the most out of the garage space you have, then you have to figure out what space is actually available. It's no good to create a plan that calls for your expensive garden tractor to be banished suddenly to the elements, when you know you want to keep it inside.

Start by waiting for a few days of good weather. Then take everything out of the garage, clean it up, and give the inside a fresh coat of paint if you want. Start putting back the things that have to stay, starting with the biggest (your cars, if you plan to keep them inside) and moving down in size. You'll quickly see this as the zero-sum game that it is. For every box of old lawn ornaments you keep, that's one less piece of exercise equipment for your new home gym. In this case, being ruthless is a virtue. Either get rid of nonessentials or find a new place to store them.

Once the essentials are back in place, you have defined the true available space with which you have to work. Now is the time to start looking for storage systems. You'll find two basic options: a cabinet-based system and a wall-hung system. Both are designed to make the most out of vertical storage.

The main difference between the two is the amount of floor space each occupies. For example, the typical base cabinet will measure about 24 inches deep, which makes it hard to fit alongside a car and still have room to open the cabinet or the car door. On the other hand, the average Peg-Board wall system projects only a few inches into the room.

Because of their different virtues, a combination of the two basic systems makes sense for filling all your needs.

Peg-Board is the granddaddy of all wall storage systems. Made of perforated hardboard into which you put metal hooks, it works as well today as it did 50 years ago.

Some storage systems blend cabinets with traditional open shelving. This shelving is very versatile and avoids the expense of cabinet doors.

Cabinet Systems

A good cabinet system is best defined by how it works, not by how it looks. If you have specialty items that are difficult to store, like some sporting goods, make sure that you find a cabinet that will handle the job. Probably the best—and the most expensive—way to get a good cabinet system is to have a cabinet dealer outfit your garage for you. However, you can do the same thing by figuring out what cabinet sizes you need and then buying knockdown units at a home center.

Another option is to buy one of the new modular garage storage systems. These systems have a big selection of different base and wall cabinets, often with a caster-mounting option so you can easily reposition the units when your needs change. Some of these manufacturers also offer wall-hung storage systems that complement their cabinets.

When looking at different cabinet lines, be sure to check for specialty units that hang from the ceiling. Some are just simple boxes with clever hanging hardware. But others are designed to make use of the entire space above your garage doors.

Increasing Your Mobility

Not everything in a garage is best stored permanently against a wall. Woodworking equipment and exercise machines are just two kinds of hardware that come to mind. These things need more space when they're being used and need much less when they're not. The logical solution is to mount them on casters so they're easy to move.

Sometimes the base of heavy-duty tools comes with holes for installing casters, but usually you'll have to create some way to mount them. This can take some time and often a lot of creativity. But once things are rolling you'll be happy you made the effort. Casters come in different sizes and with different mounting hardware. Some simply swivel, while others swivel and can be locked in place. Because you'll almost always need four casters for anything you want to move, it's a good idea to put a combination of two swivel and two locking casters on each item. This yields good maneuverability and locking capability at less cost than putting locking casters on each corner.

Modular cabinet systemsmake for very flexible storage, particularly when mounted on casters. The layout can change easily as your needs do.

Many ceiling-mounted storage units are available. Some have doors, like the one at right, others are open. Large utility units may even fit above overhead garage doors.

Wall Systems

Traditional Peg-Board is still going strong today because it's inexpensive, easy to install, and works well. But now consumers have a lot of other choices.

The most basic alternative is a shelving system that hangs from standards attached to the wall. One popular version of this is the steel-wire systems originally designed for organizing closets. With a wide variety of shelves, drawers, and compartments, you should be able to store most of what you need.

Another alternative is a modern cousin of Peg-Board: slat-wall storage systems. These slotted plastic panels are screwed directly to the garage wall, and then hooks are placed in the slots to support just about whatever you have. The system is very flexible and can easily change as your storage requirements change.

Steel-grid systems are also available. The open-grid panels are attached to the wall, and hooks and brackets are clipped onto the grid. The grids themselves are pretty inexpensive. But as with most ofthe wall storage systems, the cost of the hooks and brackets can add up quickly.

Easy-to-install and inexpensive steel-wire storage systems, originally designed for closets and kitchens, work just as well in the garage, right

Wall-hung metal shelving is a quick and clean way to get stuff off the floor, above. Most systems have wall-mounted standards and adjustable shelf brackets.

chapter 3

installing kitchen cabinets

Installing Cabinets

Installing cabinets is not difficult, but it can be an exercise in patience. Your cabinets must be installed plumb and vertical, which can be a challenge if your wall or floor is out of whack. If you find installation to be a sometimes slow but always methodical job, you're probably doing it right.

If you are adding cabinets to an existing kitchen, you will need to remove the base molding along the wall where you plan on placing the new cabinets.

Finding Studs

Wall materials such as plaster and drywall don't have the strength to support heavy cabinets. Cabinets should be supported by framing inside the wall, which usually means screwing through the wall surface into studs. Studs are typically installed on 16-inch centers, so once you've located one, you can measure along the wall to find other fastening points.

A magnetic stud finder is one of the simplest and least expensive ways to find studs. These nifty gadgets detect the nails or screws used to attach the wallboard to the wood. A bit more expensive but even better than the magnetic stud finders are the electronic stud finders now available in home centers and hardware stores.

In the absence of a stud finder, you can probe the wall with a small nail or a small-diameter bit as long as you are sure that the holes you are making will be covered by the cabinet after installation. Simply drill into the wall cavity until you hit a wall stud.

Stud finders help locate framing within a wall without damaging the surface of the wall. Most newer models use lights and sounds to indicate the location of the stud.

Finding and Marking Studs

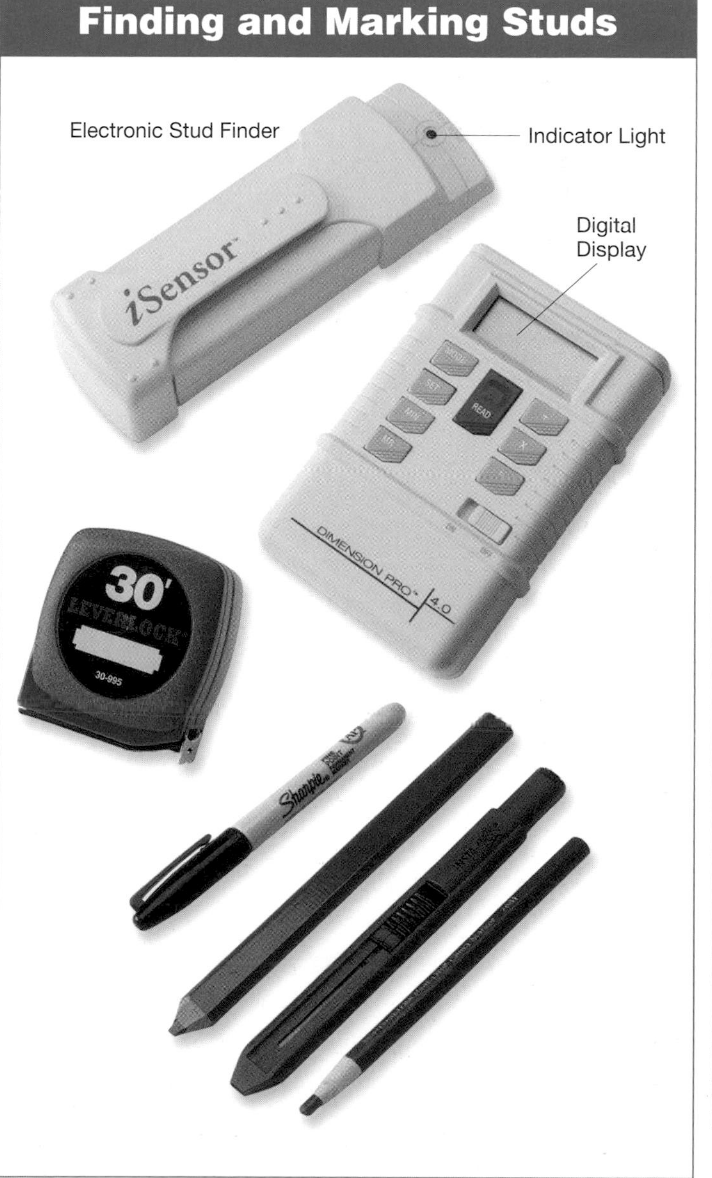

Installing Wall Cabinets

The best time to install wall cabinets is before the base cabinets are in place. Without the base cabinets taking up room, you can work close to the wall.

Your first step is to draw a level line across any wall that needs cabinets. Then install a ledger board beneath this line by driving screws into the wall studs. With a helper, lift the first cabinet into place and rest it on the ledger. Level and plumb the cabinet; then screw it to the wall.

Lift the second cabinet onto the ledger, and clamp it to the first cabinet. Screw the cabinets together through the stiles, and attach the second cabinet to the wall using screws driven through the back. Continue until all the wall cabinets are in place. Remove the ledger, and install the door hardware.

Tools & Materials

- Stud finder
- Tape measure
- Pencil
- Lumber for ledger
- 48-inch level
- Cabinets and hardware
- Wood shims
- Utility knife
- 3- and 3½-inch wood screws
- Handsaw
- Power drill-driver with assorted bits
- C-clamps or adjustable bar clamps
- Screwdrivers (flat-bladed and Phillips)

SMART TIP

Hardware Hole Jig. If you have a lot of identical hardware holes to drill in cabinet doors, make a simple cardboard template with a hole drilled at the proper place. Then hold the template against each door and bore the hole through the door.

1 Establish the proper height of the bottom of your wall cabinets, and draw a level line on the wall. Then, screw a ledger board beneath this line. Make sure the board is level and that the screws reach into the wall studs.

4 Attach the cabinets to the wall using 3-in. screws driven through the cabinet back and into the wall studs behind. Two screws at the bottom and top of each cabinet back are all that is required.

2 Start hanging the wall cabinets with a corner unit. Get some help to lift it onto the ledger board, and push it tight against the wall. One person will have to hold the cabinet until it's screwed to the wall.

3 Position the cabinet so that it is level and plumb. If necessary, use shims between the cabinet and the wall. If the first cabinet is installed plumb, the other cabinets in the row will also be plumb.

5 Lift the next cabinet onto the ledger board, and have one person hold it in place. Clamp the cabinets together at the top and bottom, and fasten them together using screws driven through the cabinet stiles.

6 Once you have joined the cabinets using screws, attach the second cabinet to the wall by driving screws through the back into the wall studs. Finish up by installing the door hardware (inset).

Installing Base Cabinets

Base cabinets are difficult to install because both the floor and the wall surface can be out of level or plumb. To correct any problems, make liberal use of cedar shimming shingles.

Start by installing the corner cabinet. Add the next cabinet in line, and shim it in place using wood shims. Be sure to check for level as you work. Screw the cabinet to the wall, and continue installing the rest of the cabinets along the wall. Finish up by installing the toe-kick boards next to the floor.

Tools & Materials

- Stud finder (or nail)
- Tape measure
- Pencil
- 1x3 ledger board
- 48-inch level
- Power drill-driver with assorted bits
- Cabinets and hardware
- Framing square
- Wood shims
- 2½-, 3-, and 3½-inch wood screws
- Handsaw
- C-clamps
- Screwdrivers
- Vinyl or wood kickplates
- Quarter-round molding

SMART TIP

Drilling Holes for Plumbing Lines. Drill holes for plumbing and waste lines before installing the cabinets. It is easier to work when the cabinets are out in the middle of the floor. Just take careful measurements of where the supply and drain lines are, and transfer these to the cabinet back.

1 Measure the height of base cabinets, and transfer this dimension to the walls. Mark a level line on the wall where the cabinets fall. Then screw ledger strips behind any corner cabinets to support the back of the countertop.

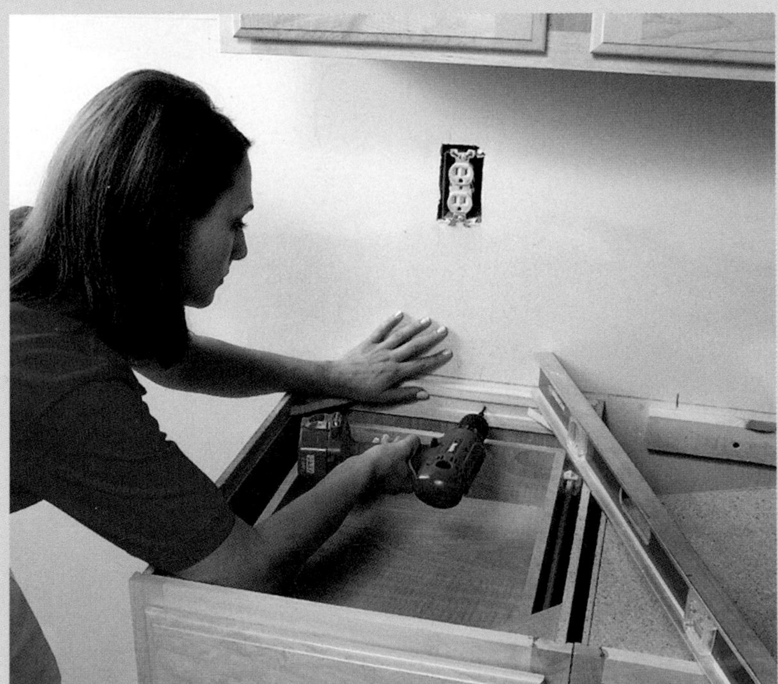

4 The next step is to screw the back of the cabinet to the wall. Just locate the wall studs, and drive screws through the back cleat and into the studs. Make sure to check level between cabinets.

2 After installing the corner cabinets, start adding the adjacent units. Make sure these are aligned square to the wall and are level and plumb. To raise the cabinet, slide wood shims underneath the sides.

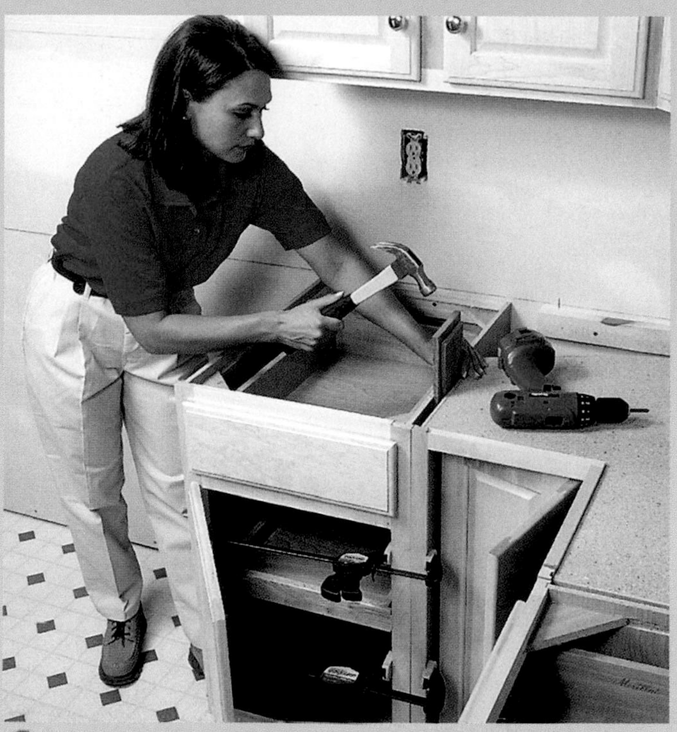

3 Also use shims between cabinets to maintain proper alignment. First, clamp the cabinet stiles together. Then install the shims, and when the fit is right, drive screws to join the stiles. Remove the clamps.

5 Once all the cabinets are installed, attach the toe-kick boards at the bottom of the cabinets. These boards will hide any gaps between the bottom of the cabinets and the floor.

Toe-Kick Heaters

Toe-kick heaters have a short profile designed to slide into the normally empty space under kitchen cabinets. They are a good solution for providing auxiliary heat when needed or to provide spot heat on particularly cold days. To install one, you will need to bring power from an existing junction box to a new switch, and pull cable from the switch to the heater—similar to the method used for installing under-cabinet lighting. Cut out the opening in the toe-kick space; then pull the cable into the room. Make the necessary electrical connections and slide the heater into position.

Installing an Island

Building a kitchen island may look complicated, but most are nothing more than a couple of base cabinets crowned with a countertop. To install one, start by drawing the outline of the island on the floor; then draw another line on the inside that represents the inside edge of the cabinet cases. Screw cleats along the inside line; lower the cabinet over the cleats; and screw the cabinets to the cleats. Cover any unfinished sides with plywood veneer set in contact cement and nailed with finishing nails. Attach the countertop base using wood screws driven from below the cabinet corner blocks, and add your finish material—plastic laminate, tile, solid surfacing—to the top. Apply trim to the corners to cover the joints; then finish up by painting or staining and finishing the veneer.

Tools & Materials

- Straightedge
- Pencil or marker
- 2x4 cleats
- Power drill-driver
- Wood/utility screws
- Base cabinets or island cabinets
- Countertop materials
- Plywood veneer
- Hammer
- Contact cement
- Finishing nails
- Wood molding
- Corner moulding

CAUTION

Most building codes require that islands be equipped with electrical outlets. Here's the reason: If you have an outlet on the island, you will not be tempted to place a countertop appliance on the island and then drape the cord across the aisle to a wall outlet, creating a potential hazard.

1 Locate the position of the island on the kitchen floor. Then, using a straightedge guide, draw an outline of the island on the floor. Draw another line, inside the first, that indicates the inside surface of the cabinet.

5 Cut the countertop base to size, and place it on the cabinets. Drive a screw up through the corner mounting blocks and into the top. Make sure that the screw doesn't break through the top of the counter.

2 Measure and cut 2x4 cleats to fit along the inside line that's drawn on the floor. Screw these down securely using 3-in. screws.

3 Lower the island cabinets over the floor cleats, and screw the bottom cabinet sides to the cleats to secure the island to the floor.

4 Cover any unfinished sides of the island with plywood veneer. Install it using contact cement and finishing nails.

6 Install cement board over the countertop base if you plan to install tile. For solid surfacing countertops, spread a bead of caulk around the perimeter of the base and lower the top in place.

7 You have many trim options for hiding the corner joints between the sides. One good one is to install wood corner molding using 4d finishing nails.

Repairing Doors and Drawers

Cabinets are not the only components in a kitchen that create a big impression. The flooring, wall coverings, paint, appliances, and furniture all make a big statement.
If you upgrade some or all of these things, you can often get by with simply cleaning and making minor repairs to cabinet doors and drawers. Fixing warped doors, replacing old drawer slides, and refinishing or replacing drawer fronts can give old cabinets a new life.

Tools & Materials

- Powdered chalk
- Block plane
- Screwdrivers
- Wood/utility screws
- Metal drawer guides

Sticking doors can often be fixed by tightening all the hinge screws. But when a door warps, it may need to be planed. Spread chalk on the door edge; then close it. Places where the chalk rubs off need stock removed. Use a block plane for best results.

Replace worn-out drawer slides with new ones. You may have to add a new rail to the inside of the cabinet to support this hardware. Once it's in place, attach one side of the slide to the cabinet and the other to the drawer side.

You can either refinish or replace drawer fronts. In both cases, remove the old ones by backing out the screws from the inside of the drawer. Attach the new ones using the same screws.

Reviving Old Cabinets

Sometimes it is not necessary or practical to replace existing cabinetry. Cabinets that are in reasonably good condition can be painted or refaced.

Painting Cabinets

A fresh coat of paint is often a good short-term solution. Begin by removing all the cabinet hardware and setting the doors and drawers aside. Fill any dents or gouges with wood filler, and when it's dry, sand it flush with the surrounding surfaces. Clean the cabinets with a strong detergent and water, and wipe them dry with an old towel. Repair and clean the doors and drawer fronts in the same way. Then sand all the exposed surfaces with 150-grit sandpaper, and wipe off all the dust with a damp rag or a tack cloth.

You'll get the smoothest finish if you spray-paint all the components. But this is usually difficult for most homeowners to do because it's hard to control the overspray. You can spray the doors and drawers in the garage or basement, but you'll generally paint the cabinets wih a brush. Just use the best-quality brush and paint you can find. Apply one coat of primer and two top coats on all the parts, sanding between coats with 220-grit sandpaper. Be sure to remove all of the sanding dust before applying the next coat of paint.

Refacing Cabinets

Refacing cabinets is a big step up from painting them. This job involves replacing the doors and drawer fronts and covering the cabinet frames and sides with wood veneer or plastic laminate that matches the doors and drawer fronts. Refacing is a good option if your existing kitchen is well designed and the cabinets are structurally sound. It costs less than half what new cabinets cost and, when combined with buying all new appliances, can dramatically change the look of your kitchen. You can do the work yourself as shown on page 38, or you can hire a contractor that specializes in refacing to handle the job.

Refacing cabinets consists of removing old doors and drawer fronts, replacing them with new ones, and covering the cabinet frames with a matching material. Refacing is a good solution for updating a kitchen that has an efficient layout.

Refacing Cabinets

Refacing cabinets is usually a job done by contractors. But experienced do-it-yourselfers can tackle it. First, prepare the cabinets as shown in this sequence; then install veneer on the side of a cabinet. Cover the stiles (the vertical sections) and rails (the horizontal sections) with flexible veneer that has pressure-sensitive adhesive on the back. Finish up by installing the doors and drawers.

Tools & Materials

- Detergent and water for cleaning
- Scraper and sandpaper
- Contact cement
- Veneer
- Laminate roller
- Router
- Utility knife
- Wood putty and putty knife
- Hinges
- Cabinet hardware and screws
- Screwdriver

1 Begin by cleaning the cabinets with detergent and water; sand all surfaces with 150-grit sandpaper, and remove the dust. Mask off adjacent surfaces up to the ends of the cabinets, and spray contact cement on the surface of the cabinet.

4 Make sure the veneer is positioned plumb on the stile; then press it down and roll it with a laminate roller. Using a utility knife, cut the veneer so that it can be wrapped around the edges.

5 Fold the veneer around the stile so that the edges are completely covered, and roll the veneer smooth using a laminate roller. Trim off any excess veneer using a utility knife and metal straightedge.

2 Cut a piece of veneer slightly larger than the cabinet side, and carefully press it into the contact cement so that there's just a slight overhang on all sides. Smooth the panel in place using a laminate roller. Trim the panel flush using a router.

3 Use flexible veneer with adhesive on the back for covering the stiles. Cut the piece to a width that covers the stile front and two side edges. Expose some of the adhesive at the top of the veneer; press it onto the stile; and then pull off the rest of the protective paper.

6 Install flexible veneer on the rail the same way as you did on the stiles. First cut it to length; then press it against the rail. Wrap the top edge, and roll the whole thing smooth. Trim the bottom edge using a utility knife.

7 Once all of the veneer is installed, fill any voids between veneer pieces with wood putty that matches the color of the veneer. Apply a finish to everything; then install the doors and drawer fronts to complete the job.

Installing Under-Cabinet Lighting

Installing fluorescent or halogen fixtures on the bottom of wall cabinets is a great way to provide task lighting for the countertop. When either type of fixture is located near the front of the wall cabinet, it completely washes the counter with light. The fixtures are also a good choice if the walls are already finished because you can install the switch and fixture with a minimal amount of damage to the wall. Place the fixture toward the front of the cabinet so that its light illuminates as much of the counter as possible. If you have framed cabinets, the face frame should shield the light. Frameless cabinets, however, usually do not offer this protection.

Plan on providing fluorescent tubes that extend about two-thirds the length of the countertop. This should provide adequate working light with no dark spots.

Tools & Materials

- Drywall saw
- Long-nose pliers
- 12/2g NM cable
- Cable stripper
- Power drill and bits
- Insulated screwdrivers
- Lighting fixture(s)
- Single-pole switch
- Wire connectors

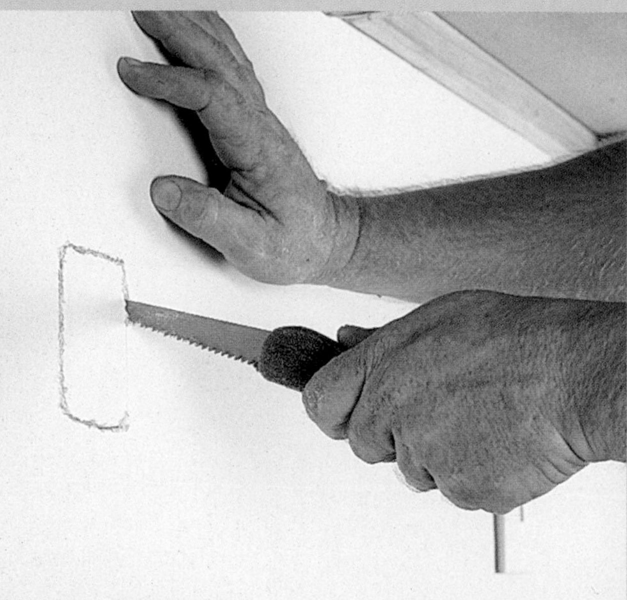

1 Start by establishing the best location for the light switch on the kitchen wall. Then trace the outline of a cut-in box on the wall. Cut along these lines using a drywall or keyhole saw.

Under-cabinet lighting improves the visibility of the countertop work area.

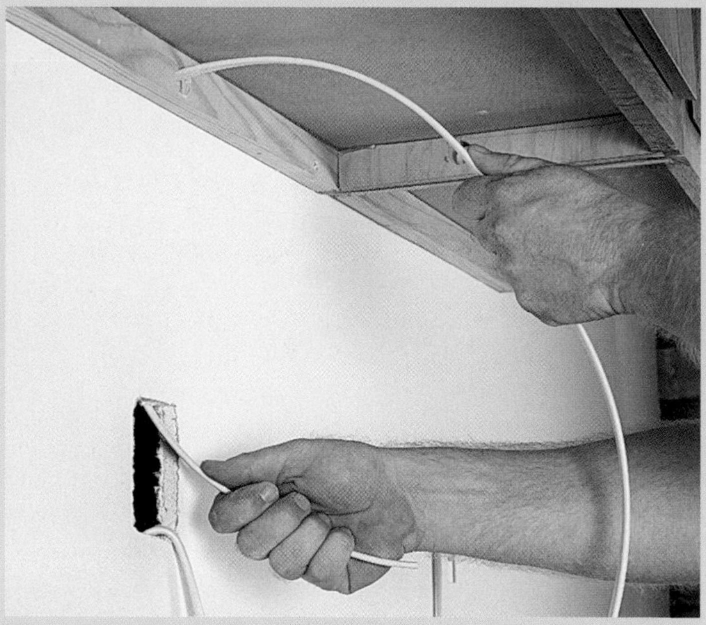

2 Once the switch-box hole is cut, fish a power cable into the hole from a close-by circuit. Make sure this circuit has enough capacity available for the lights you want to install. If it doesn't, bring a new circuit cable from the service panel. Also fish a cable from the back of a wall cabinet and into the wall opening.

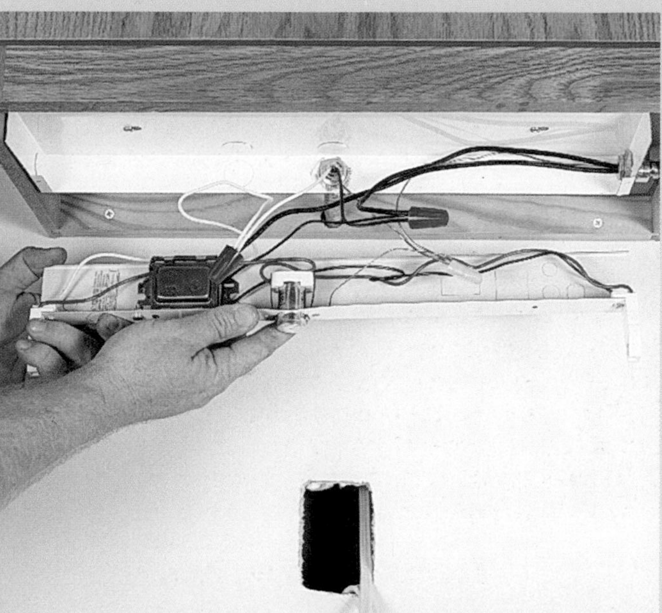

3 Attach the base of an under-cabinet fluorescent fixture to the bottom of the wall cabinet. Then pull the switch cable through a cable connector mounted in the back of the base. Tighten the connector, and join the switch wires to the fixture wires using wire connectors. Lift the light fixture onto the base, and attach it securely.

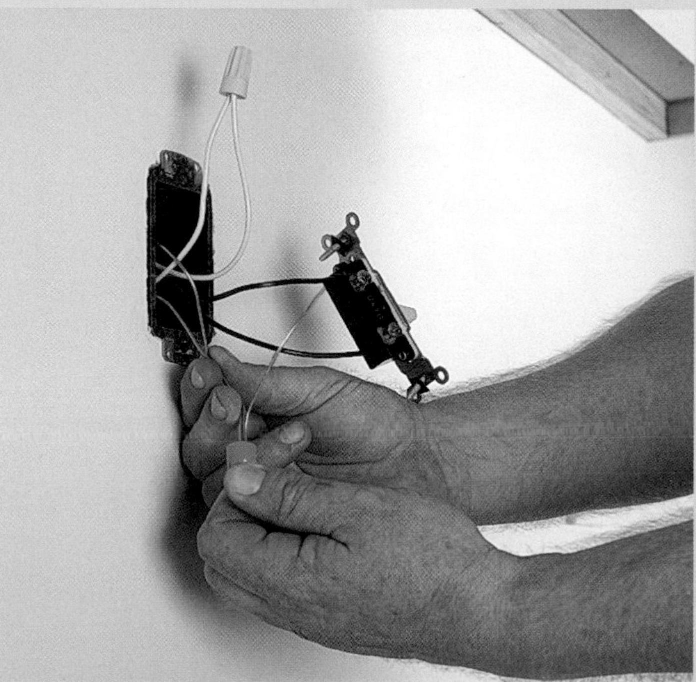

4 Install a switch box in the wall opening, and attach both black wires and a grounding wire to the switch terminals. Join the white wires together and the ground wires together using wire connectors. Screw the switch securely to the box, and test the installation.

5 If everything works correctly, install the plastic diffusers on all the fixtures. Many under-cabinet units also have surface-mounted rotary switches just behind the diffusers so that you can turn off a specific fixture while all the others stay on.

chapter 4

counters & sinks

Countertop Materials

The surfaces of your kitchen help define how it looks and determine how well it cleans up and withstands wear and tear. Choose countertops and sinks that suit your taste and lifestyle. Make sure all of these materials are easy to clean, especially the countertops. You'll spend more time cleaning these areas than you'll ever spend washing the walls or mopping the floor. The market offers lots of countertop materials, all of which are worth consideration for your kitchen. Pick the materials and designs that best suit your needs and the look of the room. You can also enhance a basic design by combining it with an eye-catching edge treatment. Another option is to combine different materials on the same surface.

Plastic Laminate. This thin, durable surface comes in hundreds of colors, textures, and patterns. The material is relatively easy to install; its smooth surface washes easily; and it is heat-resistant, although very hot pots can discolor or even burn it. Laminate stands up well to everyday wear and tear, but it can be easily scorched by hot pots and pans or scratched with knives and other sharp utensils, and surface damage is difficult to repair.

Laminate countertops are available in three forms. You can buy sheets of laminate and adhere them to a plywood base yourself. Home centers and kitchen supply dealers sell post-formed counters. These are the types that come in 8- or 10-foot lengths that you trim yourself. Both the laminate sheets and the post-form counters are available in a limited number of colors and patterns. Another option is to order a laminate counter from a counter fabricator—some home centers and kitchen dealers offer this service as well. The counter will be built to your measurements, and you will get a wide variety of colors and patterns to choose from. Most fabricators also offer a variety of edge treatments.

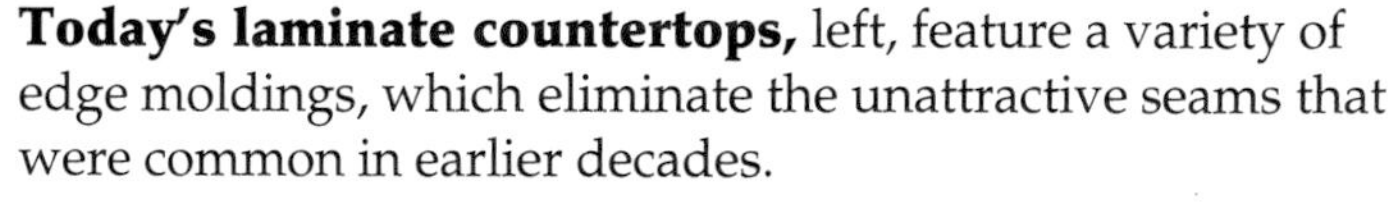

Today's laminate countertops, left, feature a variety of edge moldings, which eliminate the unattractive seams that were common in earlier decades.

Laminate countertop materials, below, are available in hundreds of colors and designs. Customize the job with a colorful backsplash.

Ceramic Tile. Glazed tile can be magnificently decorative for counters, backsplashes, and walls, or as a display inset in another material. Tile is smooth and easy to wipe clean, and it can't be burned by hot pots. In addition to the standard square tiles, ceramic tiles are available in a number of specialty shapes and sizes, allowing you to create a truly custom look. Ceramic tile costs more than laminate, but you can save money by doing the installation yourself.

When shopping, you should also consider the finish. There are two kinds: unglazed and glazed. Unglazed tiles are not sealed and always come in a matte look. They are not practical for use near water unless you apply a sealant. On the other hand, glazed tiles are coated with a material that makes them impervious to water—or spills and stains from other liquids, too. This glaze on the tile can range from matte to highly polished, depending on your taste.

The upkeep of tile is fairly easy, but you must regrout and reseal it periodically. White grout shows dirt easily, but a dark-color mix can camouflage stains. Still, unless it is sealed, grout will harbor bacteria. So clean the countertop regularly with a nonabrasive antibacterial cleanser. Tile that is well-maintained will last a lifetime, but beware: your glassware and china may not. If you drop them on this hard surface, they'll break.

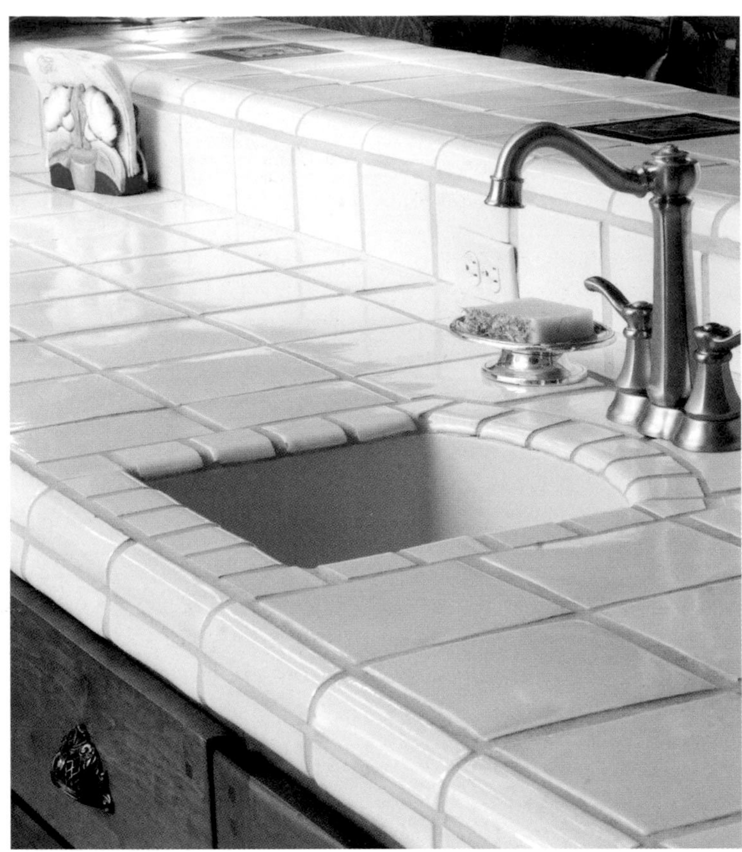

Ceramic tile, above, is a good choice for the do-it-yourself homeowner because it is easy to install. This ceramic-tile backsplash, below, ties in with the countertop's diagonal design.

The unglazed tile backsplash, above, provides a striking contrast to the polished granite countertop.

Solid-Surfacing Material. Made of acrylics and composite materials, solid surfacing comes in ½ inch and ¾ inch thicknesses. This is a premium material that resists moisture, stains, and cracks.

There is almost no limit to the colors and patterns of solid surfacing. It can be fabricated to resemble marble and granite, or it can be a block of solid color. Either way, the material can be carved or beveled for decorative effects just like wood. Manufacturers recommend professional installation.

The surface becomes scratched fairly easily, but the scratches are not readily apparent. Because the material is a solid color, blemishes (scratches, heat damage) can be removed by sanding or buffing.

Solid-surface products, above, mean just that; because they are solid, scratches can simply be sanded away.

Contrasting countertop materials, such as solid surfacing and granite, below, can work well together.

Natural Stone. Marble, slate, and granite can be formed into beautiful but expensive counters. Of the three, granite is probably the most popular because it cannot be hurt by moisture or heat, nor does it stain if finished properly. Installers polish granite to produce a high-gloss finish.

Marble scratches, cracks, and stains easily, even if waxed. Slate can be easily scratched and cracked and cannot take a high polish.

These are heavy materials that should be installed by a professional. However, you can get the look of granite and marble by installing granite or marble tiles. Cut from the natural stones, these products are available in 12 x 12-inch tiles and are installed and cut in much the same way as ceramic tiles.

Wood. Butcher block consists of hardwood laminated under pressure and sealed with oil or a polymer finish. Because it's thicker than other materials, butcher block will raise the counter level about ¾ inch above standard height. Also, wood is subject to damage by standing water or hot pans. Butcher-block tops are moderately expensive, but can be installed by amateurs.

Other kinds of wood counters may be used, especially in serving areas. Any wood used near water must be resistant to moisture or well sealed to prevent water from penetrating below the surface.

Wood may be unusual for counters but when done properly it makes a striking addition to the kitchen.

The stunning design, left, is one of many options available in engineered stone, manufactured from quartz and other natural materials.

Granite tiles are a good way to get the look of natural stone at a fraction of the cost.

Marble, above, can be expensive, so it is often used as an inset or on an island rather than to cover an entire kitchen.

Engineered stone. If you love the natural appearance and durability of granite, you might want to explore this exciting new category of man-made products. Engineered stone is manufactured primarily of quartz that is bound together with resins. It is harder than granite, requires less maintenance, and is also more heat- and bacteria-resistant. Depending upon the brand, engineered stone choices can range from subtly flecked granite lookalikes to bright primary colors. And while prices can be comparable to what you'll pay for granite, engineered stone countertops may last as long as their natural cousins.

Concrete. If your goal is to install a cutting-edge material in your kitchen, concrete is it. Thanks to new staining techniques, concrete can be saturated with color all the way through, and it can be preformed to any shape and finished to any texture. That gives kitchen designers a lot of latitude when developing custom looks. Set stone or ceramic tile chips into the surface for a decorative effect. Form it to drain off water at the sink. Be cautious, however, as a concrete countertop must be sealed, and it may crack. It's best to leave installation to a professional.

Stainless Steel. Stainless steel used for a countertop, whether it is for the entire counter or just a section of it, can look quite sophisticated, especially with a wood trim. What's practical about it is its capacity to take high heat without scorching, which makes it suitable as a landing strip for pots and pans straight from the cooktop. It is also impervious to water, so it's practical at the sink. On the negative side, stainless steel can be noisy to work on; it will show smudges; and even fingerprints can be seen easily, which never happens with other countertop materials. Depending on the grade of the material, stainless steel may also be vulnerable to scrapes, stains, and corrosion. The higher the chromium and nickel content (and therefore the grade), the better. Also, look for a thick-gauge stainless steel, which won't dent easily.

Stainless-steel countertops provide a sleek, contemporary look to any kitchen.

Concrete countertops are usually fabricated on site. They work well with other materials, as shown here.

Sinks and Faucets

The kitchen sink is the focal point in the cleanup center. This includes the sink, 18 to 24 inches of counter space on either side for dishes and food that you need to wash, a dishwasher, a waste-disposal unit (where local codes permit), and storage for glassware, frequently used utensils, detergents, colanders, and other sink accessories. The trash receptacle and recycling bins are also in the cleanup center; a trash compactor may be included here as well.

Because it's often located under a window and always tied to the plumbing system, the sink is one of the most fixed of kitchen fixtures. If you're thinking about moving your sink and dishwasher more than 60 inches from the current location, you'll probably have to rework vent and drain lines, and you might have to move a window as well. If cost containment is important to you, it's wise to begin your kitchen plan by trying to locate the sink at or near the place the old one occupies.

Where there's no window behind the sink, decide what you'll do with the wall space there. One choice is to integrate the space into a run of cabinets with units that are shorter than those on either side so that you'll have headroom. Another possibility is to install full-height cabinets only 6 inches deep. Whatever treatment you select, be sure your cleanup center includes adequate daytime and nighttime light falling directly onto the sink and adjacent counters.

Sinks

Sinks come in a great variety of sizes and shapes. Materials include stainless steel, pressed steel, cast iron, and the same solid-surfacing material used for countertops. Sinks of each material come in single-, double-, and triple-bowl models.

A single-bowl sink is large enough for soaking big pots and pans. Two-bowl sinks may have identical-size basins, or one may be smaller or shallower than the other. Three-bowl sinks include a small disposal basin at one side or between the larger bowls. These sinks usually require about 12 inches more counter space than a double-bowl unit.

How Much Counter Space?

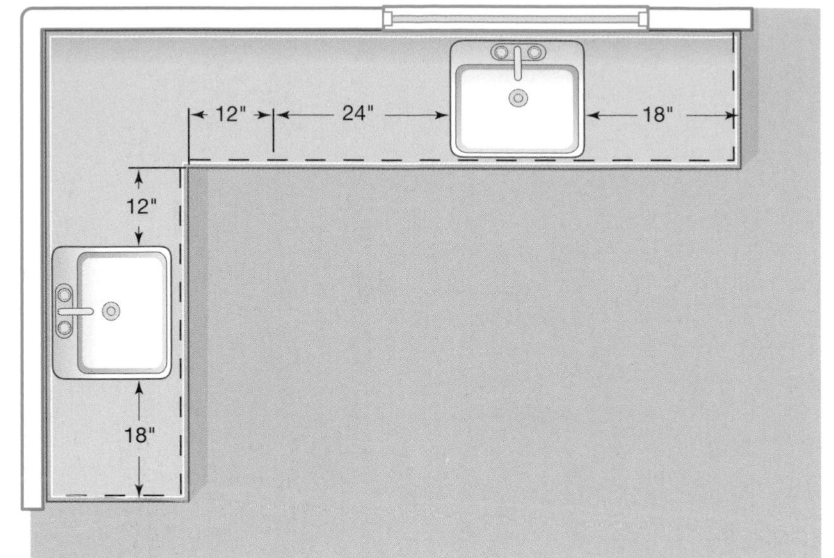

Plan adequate counter space near the main sink. For smaller second sinks, plan on 3- to 18-in. landing spaces. As with all kitchen fixtures, be sure there is enough counter space on each side of the sink. Experts recommend 18 and 24 in. of counter space.

Cleanup centers revolve around the main sink. To save money in a remodel, locate the new sink where the old one stood.

Types of Sinks

Stainless-Steel Sinks. Stainless steel, made with nickel and chrome to prevent staining, continues to be a popular choice for sinks, although some homeowners complain about spotting. This kind of sink offers the greatest selection of bowl sizes and configurations. Choose 18-gauge stainless for a large sink or one with a waste-disposal unit, lighter 20-gauge material for smaller sinks. Stainless steel also differs in grade, depending on the amount of nickel and chrome it contains. High levels of both are included in good-quality sinks.

Pressed-Steel and Cast-Iron Sinks. Both of these sinks have porcelain-enamel finishes. Cast iron is heavier and less likely to chip than pressed steel. Cast iron is also quieter than both stainless and pressed steel when water is running. These sinks are available in a wide range of colors.

Solid-Surface Sinks. Solid-surface, or acrylic, sinks can be molded directly into a solid-surface countertop, creating a seamless unit that is especially easy to keep clean. Separate drop-in models are also available. Sinks of this material are even quieter than cast iron, but costly.

Besides the common kitchen varieties, there are sinks for virtually every practical and aesthetic need—perfect circles, sinks that turn corners, deep farm-style kitchen sinks, and so on.

Stainless-steel sinks come in several sizes and configurations. Quality sinks are made of 18-gauge steel.

Under-mount sinks are attached to the underside of the counter. They work well with stone and solid-surface countertops.

Two- and three-bowl configurations are gaining popularity. This arrangement allows you to separate clean dishes from dirty ones as well as from waste materials. Some sinks come with a colander and cutting board that fits over one of the bowls. Typically, a waste-disposal unit is installed with one of the bowls, usually the larger one.

Like every other kitchen product, there are numerous options open to you. In terms of durability, any one of the materials mentioned above will hold up for years, if not decades, with the right care. Enameled cast-iron sinks tend to discolor but can be cleaned easily with a nonabrasive cleanser recommended by the manufacturer. Stainless steel and stone should be cleaned the same way. However, solid-surface sinks can take a lot of abuse. Minor scratches can be sanded out without harming the finish. You can use an abrasive agent on them. Expect a quality sink to last as long as 30 years.

Apron-front, or farmhouse, sinks have exposed fronts and are gaining popularity.

SMART TIP

In terms of installation, there are five types of kitchen sinks to consider:

- **Under-Mounted.** If you want a smooth look, an under-mounted sink may be for you. The bowl is attached underneath the countertop.
- **Integral.** As the word "integral" implies, the sink and countertop are fabricated from the same material—stone, faux stone, or solid-surfacing. There are no visible seams or joints in which food or debris can accumulate.
- **Self-Rimming or Flush-Mounted.** A self-rimmed sink has a rolled edge that is mounted over the countertop.
- **Rimmed.** Unlike a self-rimming sink, a rimmed sink requires a flat metal strip to seal the sink to the countertop.
- **Tile-In.** Used with a tiled countertop, the sink rim is flush with the tiled surface. Grout seals the sink to the surrounding countertop area.

Second Sinks

Many homeowners find that adding a second, small sink to their kitchen greatly improves the kitchen's efficiency. The primary sink is usually a full-size model that anchors the main food-preparation and cleanup areas, while the secondary sink serves outside of the major work zone. A second sink is a must when two or more people cook together routinely, but it is also handy if you practice crafts in the kitchen or entertain often and would use it as a wet bar. You can also use a secondary sink as an extra place for washing hands and the like when someone is using the main sink for preparing a meal.

Many manufacturers offer second sinks and faucets that match their full-size models. You have the same options regarding finishes, colors, styles, and the like. If you do install a second sink, you must route water, drain, and vent lines to it. Allow at least 3 inches of counter space on one side and 18 inches on the other.

Two-sink kitchens can make cooking more efficient.

Faucets

State-of-the-art technology in faucets gives you not only much more control over water use, but better performance and a wider selection of faucet finishes as well. Features to look for include pullout faucet heads, retractable sprayers, hot- and cold-water dispensing, single-lever control, anti-scald and flow-control devices, a lowered lead content in brass components, and built-in water purifiers to enhance taste.

For a quality faucet, inquire about its parts when you shop. The best are those made of solid brass or a brass-base material. Both are corrosion-resistant. Avoid plastic components—they won't hold up. Ask about the faucet's valving, too. Buy a model that has a washerless cartridge; it will cost more, but it will last longer and be less prone to leaks. This will save you money in the long run.

Besides selecting a spout type (standard, arched, gooseneck, or pullout), you may choose between single or double levers. Pullout faucets come with a built-in sprayer. Others require installing a separate sprayer. Until recently, a pressure-balanced faucet (one equipped with a device that equalizes the hot and cold water coming out of a faucet to prevent scalding), came only with single-lever models. Now this safety feature is available with faucets that have separate hot- and cold-water valves. You may mix your spout with one of many types of handle styles: wrist blades, levers, scrolls, numerous geometric shapes, and cross handles. If your fingers or hands get stiff, choose wrist blades, which are the easiest to manipulate.

Chrome, brass, enamel-coated or baked-on colors, pewter, and nickel are typical faucet finishes. Some finishes, such as chrome, are easier to care for than others; brass, for example, may require polishing. Technologically advanced coatings can make even delicate finishes, such as the enameled colors, more durable unless you use abrasive cleaners on them, which will scratch the finish. You may expect a good-quality faucet to last approximately 15 years; top-of-the-line products will hold up even longer.

Pot fillers save you steps to the sink while cooking. Choose one that can reach most of the burners on your cooktop.

Types of Faucets

- **High Gooseneck.** Gooseneck spouts facilitate filling tall pitchers and vases and make pot cleaning easier when the sink bowl is shallow. This faucet type is great at a bar sink or auxiliary food preparation sink for cleaning vegetables.
- **Single Lever.** One lever turns on and mixes hot and cold water. Styles range from functional to sleek.
- **Double-Handle Faucet.** Temperature may be easier to adjust with separate hot and cold controls. Most contain washers and seals that must occasionally be replaced.
- **Single-Handle Faucet with Pullout Sprayer.** A pullout faucet allows single-handed on, off, temperature control, and spraying.
- **Pot Fillers**. Pot fillers are mounted to the wall over the cooktop. Some versions have a pullout spout. Others feature a double- or triple-jointed arm that can be bent to reach up and down or swiveled back and forth, allowing the cook to pull the faucet all the way over to a pot on the farthest burner of a wide commercial range.

Don't be sidetracked by how good today's sinks and faucets may look. The products you ultimately select must not only be attractive but also function well in your new kitchen. As a practical matter, compare the size of your biggest pots and racks to see whether the sink and faucet you are considering will accommodate them. You may be able to compensate for a shallow sink by pairing it with a pullout or gooseneck faucet. But a faucet that is too tall for a sink will splash water; one that is too short won't allow water to reach to the sink's corners. If you plan a double- or triple-bowl sink, the faucet you select should be able to reach all of the bowls.

Countertop Options

There are a number of countertop options available to you, including laminate, ceramic tile, solid surfacing, natural stone, stainless steel, and concrete. Of this list, laminate and ceramic tile counters are best suited for the do-it-yourselfer because the tools and materials are widely available. Setting a solid-surface countertop in place is relatively easy, but fabricating the actual countertop requires skill and expertise. Besides, most manufacturers deal only with professional countertop fabricators and installers.

If you have decided on a laminate countertop, you can fabricate one yourself by attaching the laminate to a substrate or by purchasing a prefabricated countertop that you install. There have always been ready-made countertops available in standard lengths that you cut to fit your needs. Called post-formed countertops, they come with integral rounded backsplashes and are available in a limited range of colors. (See "Installing a Prefab Countertop," page 54.) But an increasing number of home centers and dealers are serving as the middle men between countertop fabricators and homeowners. You can order a countertop cut to your specifications in any one of a wide range of laminate colors and textures. You can also specify edge treatments. If you go this route, have the retailer or fabricator take the measurements for the countertop. That way, if the countertop doesn't fit, the fabricator is responsible for fixing the problem.

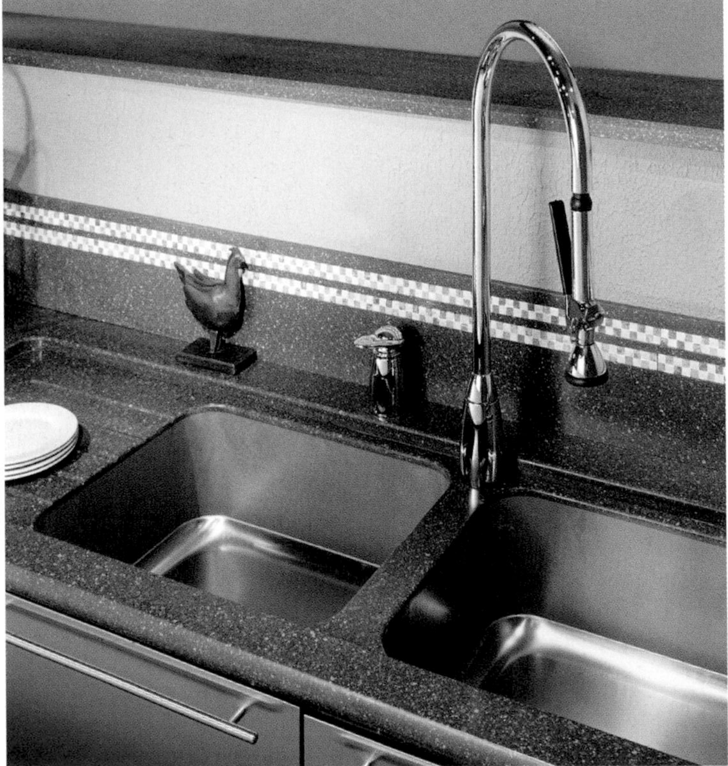

Solid-surface countertops are installed by professional countertop fabricators. Each one is custom made.

Making a Laminate Countertop

Plastic laminate is a durable, affordable, and attractive countertop finish material. It's available in solid colors, patterns, and metallic-coated sheets, to name just a few design options. Working with it requires some special skills. But compared with other counter materials, such as natural stone or solid surfacing, building a laminate countertop is a breeze.

Start by building the countertop substrate using either ¾-inch-thick exterior-grade plywood or particleboard. A double layer is best, but a single layer with the edges built up with 4-inch-wide strips is acceptable. Join the layers using carpenter's glue and drywall screws.

Begin applying the plastic laminate to the edges of the substrate. Use contact cement, and make sure to roll all the pieces flat with a laminate roller. Install the top sheet as shown below in step 4; then trim the edges flush with a router and a bevel bit with a ball-bearing guide.

Tools & Materials

- ¾-inch plywood and cement backer board (optional)
- Laminate
- Gloves, eye protection, and respirator
- Contact cement and brush
- Laminate roller
- Brown wrapping paper or lattice strips
- Router with carbide flush-trimming bit and roller-guided bevel bit

CAUTION

Be sure to use contact cement only in well-ventilated areas. Exposure to its fumes can irritate your nose, throat, and lungs. Be sure to wear eye protection and rubber gloves as well.

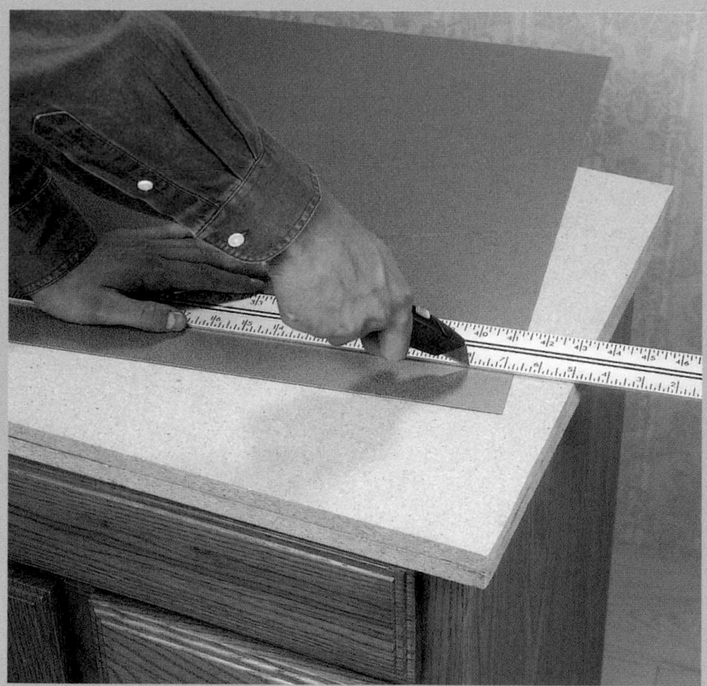

1 Start by cutting the laminate for the countertop edges. You can rough cut these pieces using a sharp utility knife. Just use it, with a metal straightedge, to score the back of the sheet. Then snap the sheet along the score line. You can also use a laminate scoring tool for this job.

2 You'll glue laminate to the countertop substrate using contact cement. Spread the adhesive on both mating surfaces; allow to dry a bit; and then press the parts together. Use a disposable paintbrush, and wear gloves, eye protection, and a respirator to avoid breathing the fumes.

3 Once the cement has set properly, carefully align the edge laminate and push it in place. Roll it smooth with a laminate roller, and trim all the edges using a router and a flush-trimming bit.

4 Place lattice strips on the counter, and lower the laminate onto them. Make sure the sheet overhangs on all sides. Pull out the strips one at a time, and press down on the sheet.

5 Using the laminate roller, roll the sheet across the top of the counter to make a complete bond. Then cut off the overhanging edges using a router and a roller-guided bevel bit.

Installing a Prefab Countertop

Prefabricated countertops, also called post-formed countertops, are stock units at the large chain home centers. You just buy one that looks good to you and is the right size. Installing these tops is usually easy. First make sure the base cabinets are level; then lower the top in place; scribe its backsplash to the wall; attach it to the cabinets; and caulk around its perimeter. These tops can be cut to any length and mitered to form right angles.

Tools & Materials

- 48-inch level
- Countertop
- Shims (if necessary)
- Power drill-driver and assorted bits
- Sandpaper or file
- Belt sander
- Wood screws as needed
- Caulking gun and adhesive caulk
- Iron (optional)

1 Before installing the countertop, check the cabinets for level from side-to-side and front-to-back. Use a 4-ft. level for the most accurate results. If necessary, shim the cabinets until all are aligned.

4 To place the countertop, get a couple of helpers to lift it and lower it onto the cabinets. Make sure that one person supports any joint in the top to reduce the bending stress.

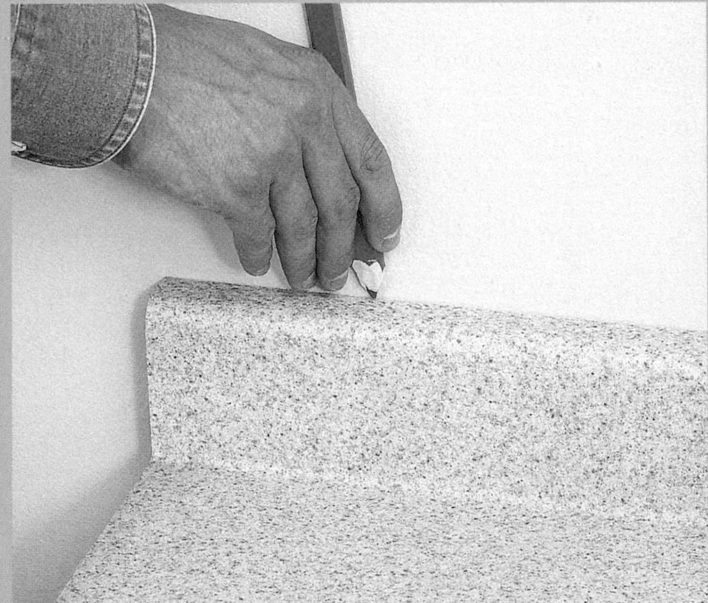

5 Push the top against the wall, and carefully scribe the backsplash to the wall using a wide, flat carpenter's pencil. Remove the top, and sand the back of the backsplash so that it conforms to the scribe line. A belt sander works well for this job, but it creates a lot of dust. Be sure to wear a dust mask when using one.

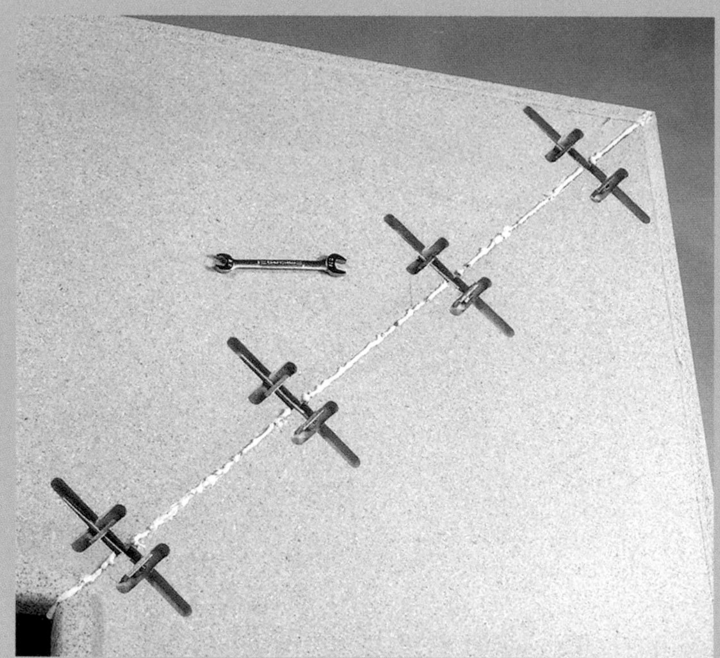

2 Corner joints, like the mitered joint above, are joined with adhesive and I-bolts. You order the counter sections with the miter and the T-slots (for the I-bolts) already cut. Spread the adhesive; then insert the bolts and slowly tighten them. Keep the sections aligned as they are drawn together.

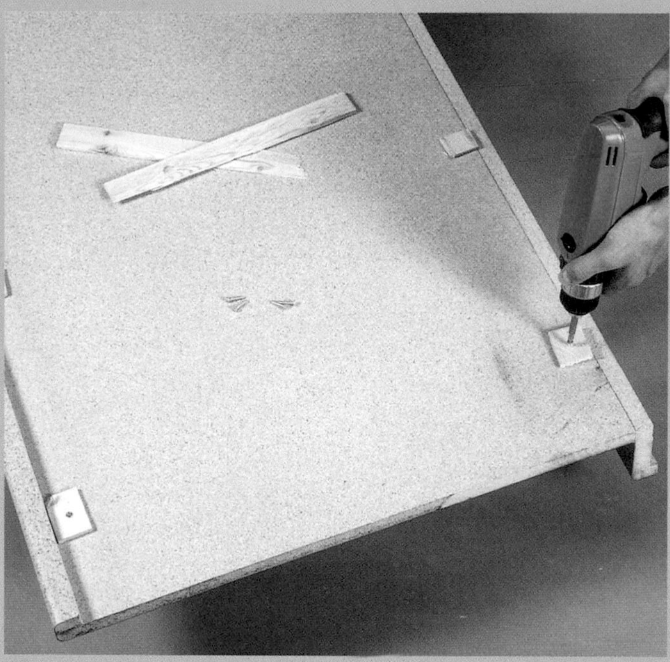

3 Before putting the top in place, check the height of the cabinets. If they aren't at least 34½ in. high (which is the rough-in clearance for most under-counter appliances), then cut and screw small riser blocks to the back and front edges of the top to yield more clearance.

6 The countertop is held to the cabinets by screws driven up through the cabinet corner blocks and into the underside of the top. Don't use screws that are long enough to break through the surface of the top.

7 Once the top is screwed to the cabinets, use silicone caulk to fill the seam where the backsplash meets the wall. This caulk will prevent moisture from getting behind the top.

8 On exposed countertop ends, install preformed end strips that match the top laminate. These strips usually are coated with a heat-activated adhesive. Use a hot clothes iron to press the strip in place.

Installing Backer Board for Tile

The key to a good tile job is to create a stable base that won't move. If the base does move, it can easily cause cracked grout and even broken tiles. The best approach is to start with a ¾-inch-thick plywood substrate and then cover this with a layer of ½-inch-thick cement-based backer board. Maintain ⅛-inch-wide gaps between panels, and fill these with thinset mortar and fiberglass mesh tape.

Tools & Materials

- Lumber for reinforcing strips
- Construction adhesive
- Caulking gun
- Exterior-grade plywood
- Power drill-driver and bits
- Square ▮ Template
- Saber saw
- 4-mil polyethylene
- Stapler
- Notched trowel
- Thinset adhesive
- Backer board ▮ Utility knife
- Fiberglass mesh tape

1 Install backer board over an exterior-grade plywood substrate using 4-in.-wide perimeter reinforcing strips. Once you have fabricated the substrate, run a bead of construction adhesive along the top edges of all the cabinets, and lower the plywood top in place.

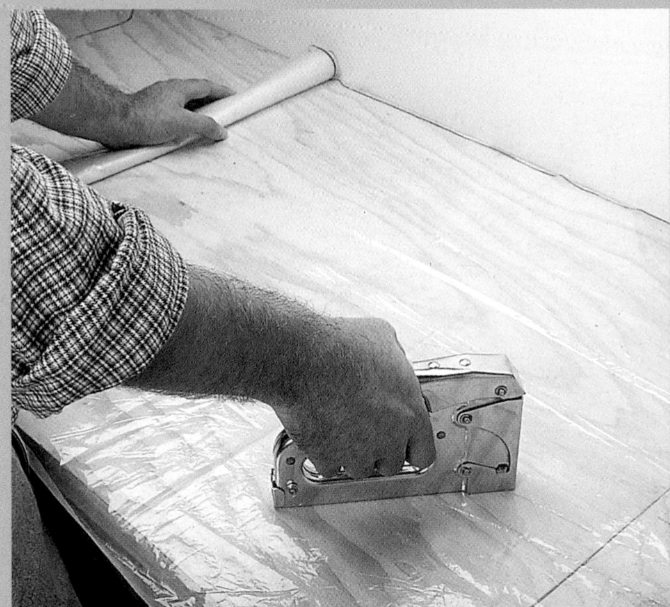

4 Apply a moisture barrier to the plywood substrate top. Use a sheet of 4-mil polyethylene or 15-lb. roofing felt. Keep the barrier smooth, and staple it in place with ¼-in.-long staples. Make sure that all the staples are driven completely into the top and not sticking up.

5 Using a notched trowel, spread thinset adhesive over the entire plywood top. Then cut ½-in.-thick backer-board panels to size and lower them into the thinset. Leave a space of about ½ in. between any abutting panels.

2 Hold the countertop in place with screws driven up through cabinet corner blocks into the underside of the top. Measure to make sure you use the right-size screws and not ones that are not so long that they extend through the top surface of the plywood.

3 Before installing any cement backer board, you have to make a cutout in the plywood for the sink. Put the template that comes with the sink onto the top, and trace it according to the manufacturer's instructions. Be sure to keep the template square to the front edge of the counter. Cut out the sink opening, and test the sink for fit.

6 Install backer-board panels up to the sides of the sink cutout, using corrosion-resistant screws. Add narrow strips along the front and back of the sink cutout to fill those voids. Make sure that you maintain a ⅛-in.-wide space between all the pieces of backer board.

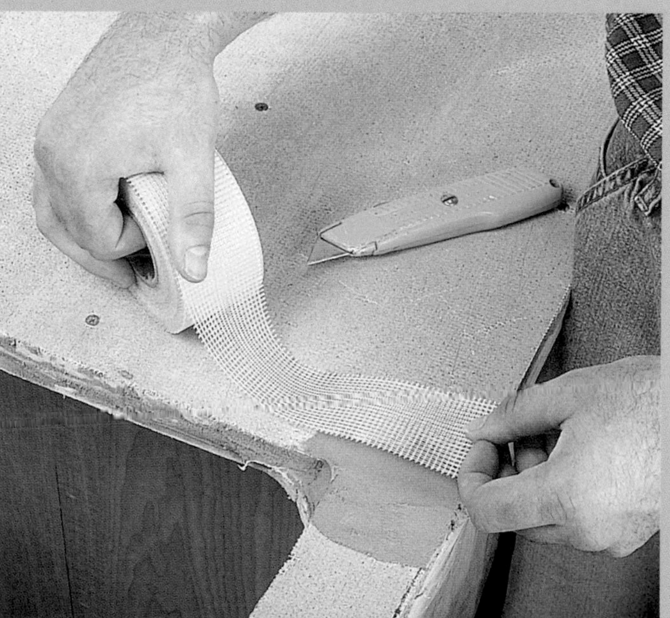

7 Fill the gap between any panels with thinset adhesive, and trowel the surface smooth. Then embed fiberglass mesh tape over all the joints, and carefully trowel it smooth. Once the backer-board adhesive dries, lightly sand the entire top with 100-grit sandpaper and a sanding block to make sure it is smooth.

Backsplash Options

Rounded Edge (Bullnose)
Thinset
Drywall
Caulk

Cap
Grout
Thinset
Backer Board
Drywall
Caulk

Trim Tile
Grout
Thinset
Drywall
Cove Tile
Caulk

One of these three designs can be used to create a simple tile backsplash. Only the center option requires a backer board or plywood substrate. Be sure to caulk the joint between the field tiles and the vertical backsplash.

Great-Looking Granite

Granite countertops are usually installed by professionals, but you can get the same look by installing granite tiles. The installation procedure is similar to the one shown opposite. Use special granite and marble mortar rather than tile thinset. Seal the stone before grouting to prevent staining.

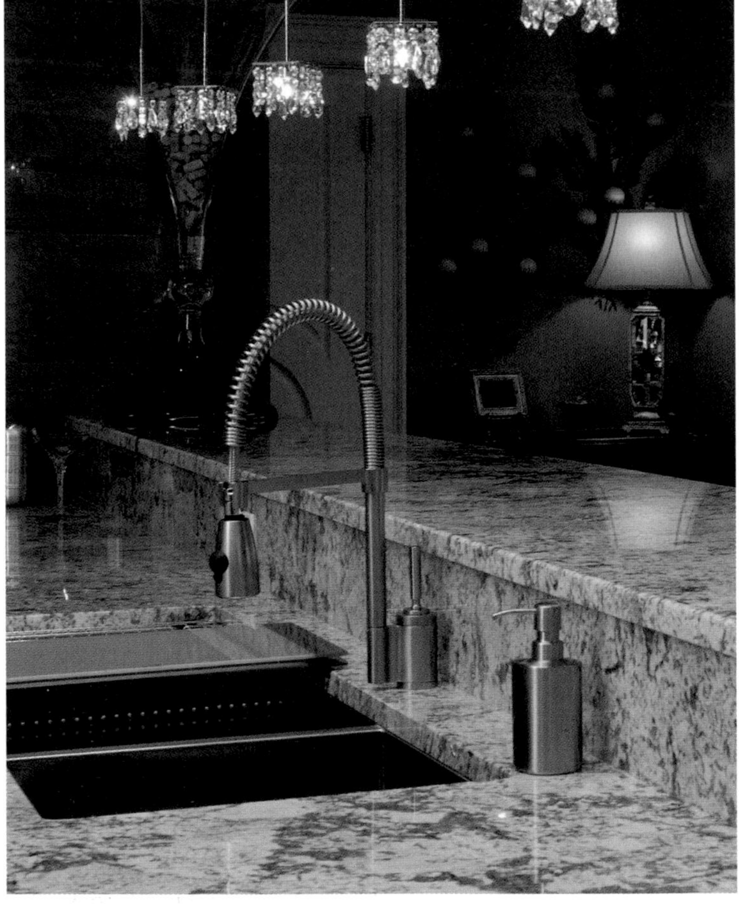

This granite counter, backsplash, and matching breakfast bar provide a look of seamless elegance to this open kitchen.

Tiling a Countertop

Once your countertop substrate is prepared, take the time to dry fit the tile. Lay out all the field tile, and check for satisfactory appearance. Usually, starting with a full tile at the front of the counter and cutting the tiles along the wall will look best because these partial tiles will almost always be covered with small appliances and other things. It's also a good idea to use full tiles alongside the sink or other countertop cutouts.

Tools & Materials

- Chalk-line box
- Ceramic tiles
- Carpenter's pencil
- Tile adhesive
- Notched trowel
- Plastic spacers
- Tile cutters
- Putty knife
- Masking tape
- Tile grout
- Rubber float
- Sponge

1 Start the tile layout by holding an edge tile to the edge of the substrate, and mark the back of the tile on the top. Snap chalk lines at these marks; then spread adhesive on the top using a notched trowel (inset). The chalk lines will show through the adhesive.

2 Starting at the chalk lines, lay the field tiles using small plastic spacers between the tiles. Periodically check the surface of the tiles to make sure each is lying flat. High spots can be pushed down with gentle hand pressure.

3 After all the full tiles have been set, begin marking the partial tiles for cutting. Hold the partial tile over a full tile, and mark the length. Allow for the grout gap between the tiles; then cut the full tile using a tile cutter, and place it on the top so the cut edge faces the wall.

4 Apply adhesive to the edge of the countertop using a notched trowel. Then cover the back of the trim tile with adhesive using a putty knife. Make sure both surfaces of the tile are completely covered with adhesive. Use masking tape to hold trim tiles in position if necessary.

5 Install the tile. Allow to cure overnight. Then, using a rubber float, work grout into all joints. Work across the tiles to embed grout. Remove haze by wiping with a barely damp sponge. Wet and wring out the sponge frequently as you work.

Sink Options

The installation method you choose not only depends on the type of sink you purchase but also on the countertop. Laminate and ceramic-tile countertops consist of substrates that cannot be exposed, so the sink should rest on the countertop. For these countertops choose either a self-rimming or metal-rim sink. Solid surfacing and natural stone are not necessarily installed on substrates, and their edges may be exposed. This gives you the opportunity to install an undermount sink.

Installing a Rimmed Sink

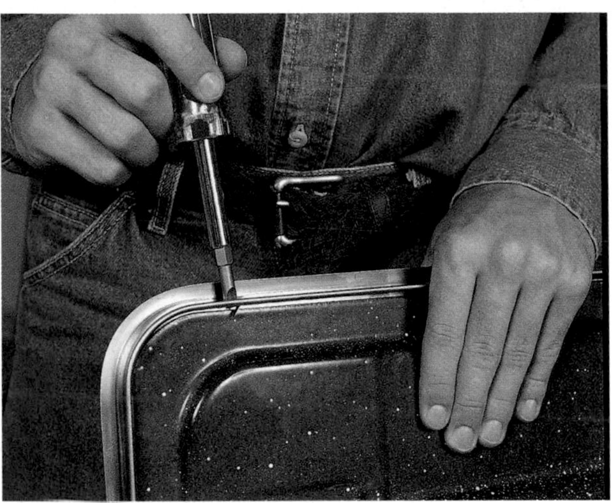

1. Set the rim over the sink, and use a screwdriver to bend the tabs inward on the sink rim. With a cast-iron sink, install supporting corner brackets.

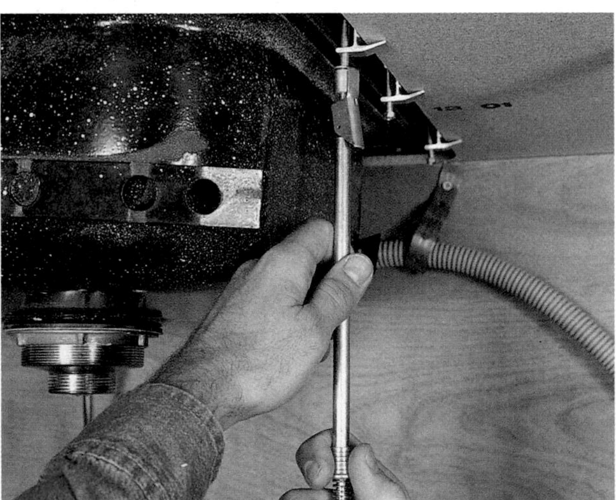

2. Use a sink-clip wrench (or a long nut driver or screwdriver) to drive the clip bolts against the underside of the countertop. Space clips about 8 inches apart. If the corners do not draw down, use an extra clip at each corner.

Installing a Self-Rimming Sink

Self-rimming sinks are installed so they sit on top of the counter. Cast-iron models, like the one shown here, are heavy enough so that once installed they won't move. But lighter models will have clips that must be added after the sink is lowered into the hole. The hardest part of the job is cutting the hole in the countertop. Just take your time while cutting, and be sure to use a new, sharp blade in your saber saw.

Tools & Materials

- Template
- Saber saw
- Power drill-driver with bit
- Utility knife
- Sink
- Caulking gun
- Silicone caulk
- Gloves
- Drain kit
- Plumber's putty
- Spud wrench or groove-joint pliers

3 Place the sink upside down on the counter, and run a fat bead of silicone caulk around the underside of the sink rim. When the caulking is done, install the faucet and spray hose, which is much easier to do when the sink is inverted.

1 Many sinks come with a template that makes locating the sink opening easy. Just tape it to the countertop, and trace around its perimeter. If your sink doesn't have a template, invert your sink on the top; trace around its edge; and mark the cut line inside this traced line, following the manufacturer's instructions.

2 To cut the sink opening, begin by drilling blade-entry holes at all four corners. Then make the side cuts with a saber saw. Work slowly, and hold the saw firmly to keep it from bouncing up and down, which can scratch the countertop.

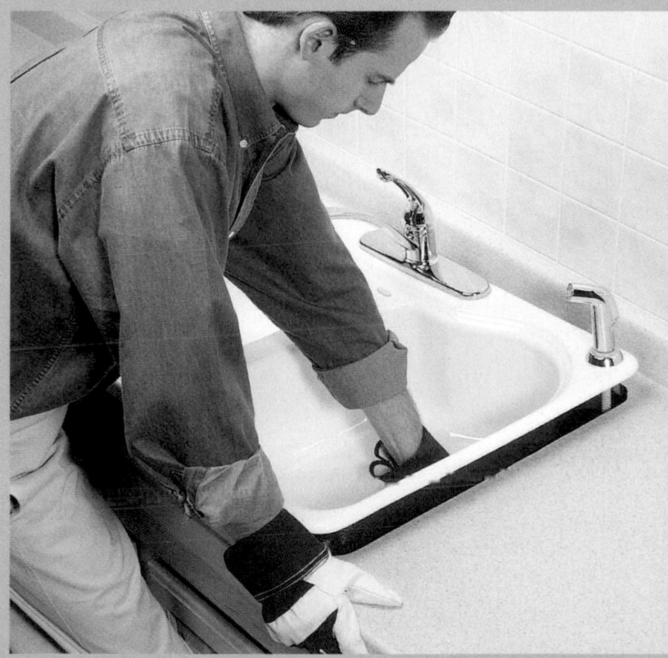

4 Carefully lower the sink into the opening by holding it in the drain hole. Check the sink for proper alignment, and adjust as necessary. For heavy sinks, like this cast-iron model, the weight of the sink combined with the silicone caulk will keep the sink from moving.

5 It's usually best to install the drain hardware after the sink is in place. First, spread an ample roll of plumber's putty on the underside of the drain flange; then push the flange into place from above. Hold the gaskets in place, and thread the spud nut onto the drain piece. Tighten the nut.

Hooking Up a New Faucet and a New Sink

Each manufacturer has slightly different requirements for installation, but the basics connections remain the same. In most cases, it is best to mount the faucet in the sink before you install it in the countertop because it is easier to secure the faucet to the sink before the fixture is in place. Shown here is a faucet with a pullout spray that requires a supply adapter that connects to the hose.

Tools & Materials

- New faucet
- Screwdriver
- Groove-joint pliers
- Latex tub-and-tile caulk
- PVC trap and drain line
- Supply risers, compression fittings
- Pipe-joint compound

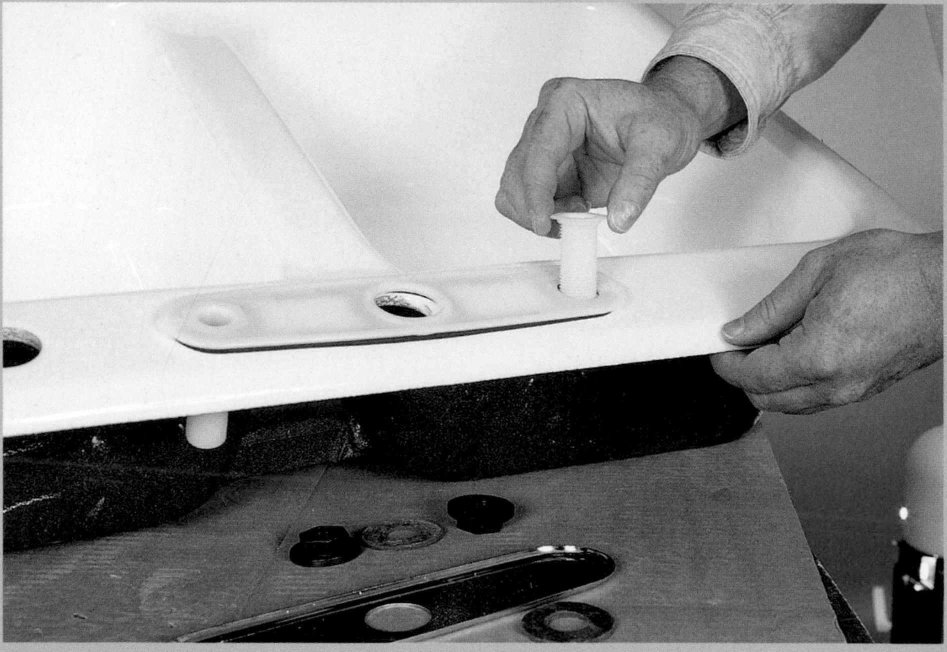

1 With the sink resting on a work surface (either the countertop covered by cardboard or a separate surface entirely), place the faucet's base plate over the deck holes. This is a single-column faucet, but it can be installed in a sink with three holes as shown here. The base plate will cover the holes. Install the plastic jamb nuts on the shanks that protrude below the sink. Make the nuts finger-tight.

4 This faucet has a pullout spray in the spout and requires a supply adapter that is attached under the sink. Install the adapter on the faucet nipple. Most faucets use a slip fitting with an O-ring seal. With the adapter on the nipple, thread the spray hose onto the adapter. Tighten until the attachment feels snug.

5 From above, thread the outlet end of the spray onto the hose. Pull the hose out several feet to test. Make sure the drain assembly is in place as shown on page 61.

2 Snap the decorative base plate over the plastic support. The base plate should be parallel with the back edge of the sink. Straighten the plumbing lines on the faucet, and insert the faucet body into the middle hole in the sink deck.

3 Slide the mounting hardware onto the column, and thread the hardware up the shank of the faucet. This model has a plastic spacer, a steel washer, and set screws. When the assembly is snug against the bottom of the sink, tighten the set screws using a screwdriver.

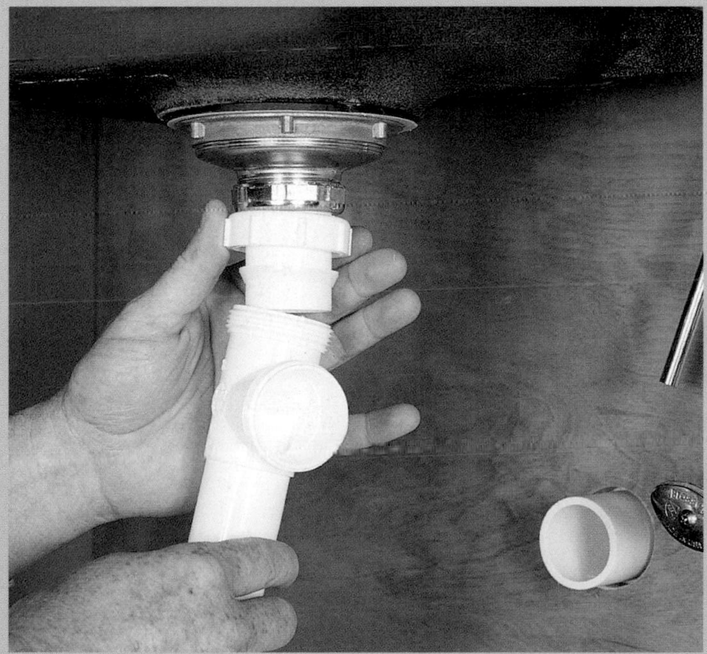

6 A short tailpiece attached to the drain by a chrome nut connects the drain to the trap assembly. This photo shows a T-fitting that connects the trap to a second sink. For single-bowl sinks, use a tailpice without the fitting, and attach it to a P-trap. Connect this assembly to the drain line.

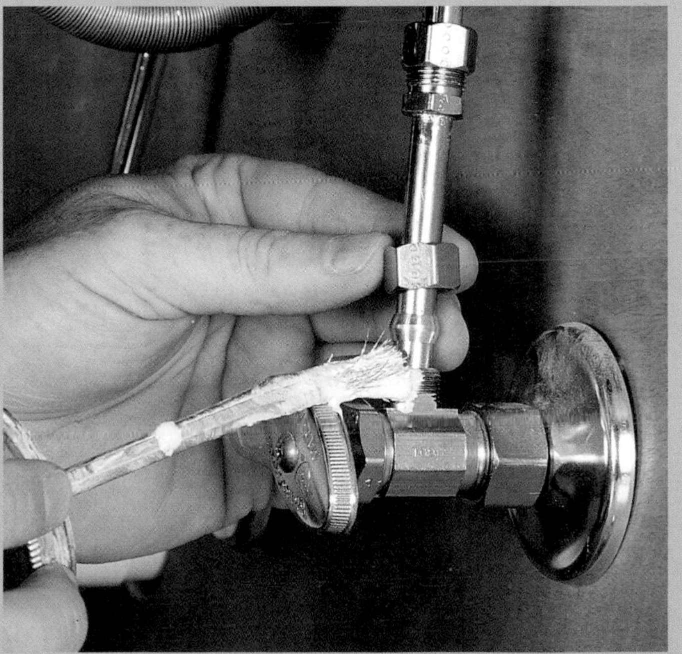

7 To complete the job, hook up the water-supply risers to the shutoff valves. Cut the risers to size if necessary. Connect each riser to the faucet and to the corresponding shutoff valve. Here, compression fittings are used to make the connection. Coat the threads and ferrule with pipe-joint compound. Tighten the compression nuts.

chapter 5

appliances

Dealing with Appliances

Appliances tend to be the 800-pound gorillas in rooms where they appear. The devices are usually big and heavy, and they often require water, waste, and vent hookups that work better in some locations than others, so it makes sense to plan for the locations of the appliances first and then add the cabinets and counters around them.

Start by finding out the installation requirement of each appliance. You will need to know the dimensions of the appliances and whether they have special requirements, such as a gas line, a water source, or a high-capacity electrical circuit.

If you're installing cabinets in a kitchen, which will have multiple appliance locations, then use the traditional work triangle to create a design framework. The work triangle refers to the placement of the main sink, the range, and the refrigerator. These should form a triangle with three sides that total at least 12 feet but no more than 26 feet. These distances make for an efficient work environment, with short walks between the three appliances and enough counter space along the way to drop off groceries and cut up vegetables. Then plan the cabinets based on the work area.

Some large kitchens that have a separate oven and cooktop, multiple sinks, or a freezer drawer in addition to a refrigerator may require a secondary work triangle to reflect the way you'll work in these larger rooms.

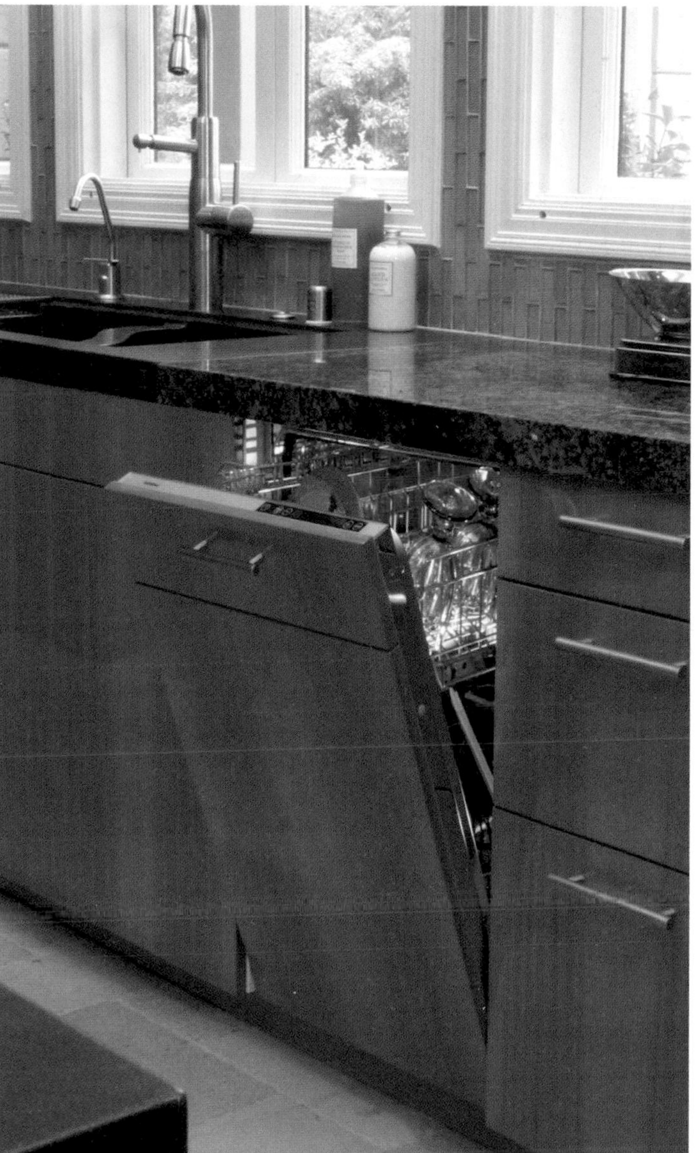

Refrigerator drawer units, left, provide the ultimate in built-in looks. They are designed to fit under standard-height countertops.

Built-in dishwashers, above, are usually 24 in. wide. Install them between two base cabinets.

Food Preparation

Preparing food requires fire and ice. Luckily for us in the modern world, these are provided by a wide choice of functional and beautiful appliances: the ice by refrigerator/freezers, of course, and the fire by cooktops and ovens.

Refrigerators and Freezers

Refrigerators vary by size, which affects how they look with your cabinetry. Many refrigerators require a space that extends out beyond the full depth of a base cabinet and upward into the overhead cabinet space. In recent years, however, manufacturers have been offering 25-inch-deep freestanding models, which do not protrude too far beyond the front edges of counters. Built-in 24-inch-deep designs further minimize the bulk of this massive piece of kitchen equipment. Shallower refrigerators and freezers are wider than standard models, however, and often taller as well, so allocate kitchen space accordingly.

When placing refrigerators in a kitchen design, plan to have open counter space on both sides of the unit as landing space when cooking or when loading the unit after shopping.

Shopping Tips

To estimate the refrigerator/freezer capacity your family needs, allow 12 cubic feet of total refrigerator and freezer space for the first two adults in your household; then add 2 more cubic feet for each additional member. Typically, a family of four would need a refrigerator/freezer with a capacity of 16 cubic feet. You must increase this capacity, however, if you prepare meals for the week in advance and keep them in the refrigerator or freezer. If your teenagers down a half-gallon of milk in a swallow, increase milk storage capacity.

Food-preparation centers require a range or cooktop, above, and a refrigerator, below. Note how the range, refrigerator, and sink are within easy reach of one another.

Refrigerators & Counters

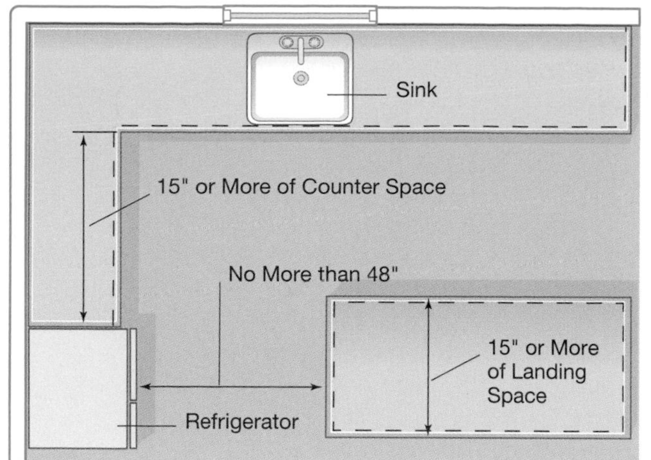

Plan adequate counter space near refrigerators. Island landing space should be no more than 48 inches away.

Cool Options for Refrigerators

Today refrigerators can be loaded with options unheard of even a few years ago. As with any purchase, extras tend to drive up the price of the appliance, but many options can make your life easier or the appliance more efficient. Here are some to consider:

- Adjustable shelving
- Automatic ice maker
- Automatic defroster
- Wine rack
- Through-the-door water and ice dispenser
- Extra-deep door shelves for gallon jugs
- Zoned temperature controls
- Separate controls for crisper drawers
- Slide-out shelves and leak-proof shelves
- The ability to accept panels that match cabinets

If you freeze produce from your garden for use out of season, increase your freezer space or consider buying an additional standalone freezer. Most conventional refrigerators come in one of these styles:

Top Freezer. The freezer and refrigerator sections are separate, usually with automatic defrosting. The freezer will maintain food for long periods of time.

Bottom Freezer. Similar in look to top-mounted freezer units, bottom mounts have a large freezer section under the main refrigerator area. Newer models have side-by-side doors on the upper refrigerator compartment.

Side-by-Side. A side-by-side offers the greatest access to both compartments and requires the least door-swing clearance in front. Side-by-side models are wider than up-and-down versions, and their narrow shelves may not handle bulky items, such as a large frozen turkey.

Modular. Modular refrigerators offer a departure from the vertical box we're used to. This concept allows refrigerator or freezer drawer units and cabinets to be located strategically throughout the kitchen—or house. The units are only 27 inches wide and are standard cabinet depth. They accept all types of paneling and handles, so they can blend in with cabinetry. Drawer units and cabinets may be individually temperature-controlled for optimal food storage—32 to 34 degrees F for vegetables, 38 degrees for milk, and 30 to 32 degrees for meats.

Under-counter-style refrigerators, freezers, and combination units provide for some specialized needs—such as keeping wine at the right temperature.

Wine coolers keep your favorite vintages at optimal temperature.

Modular drawer units can be placed throughout the kitchen.

Cooking Center

The term "cooking center" may sound a bit grand, but with all of the options available, including restaurant-style ranges, modular cooktops, microwaves, and convection ovens, many home chefs want more than just a set of burners with an oven underneath.

The cooking center refers to the cooking appliance and the countertops and cabinets that surround it—or are within easy reach. Plan for open working space on both sides of the cooktop or range. Plan cabinets and drawer units that hold pots and pans, cooking utensils, and spices and other ingredients you use often.

Ranges

Until the late 1950s, the heart of every American kitchen was a "stove" that stood off by itself so heat would not damage nearby cabinets and countertops. Today the successors to the stove are drop-in or slide-in ranges that are insulated at the sides and rear so that they can fit flush against cabinets and other combustible surfaces. The most common range styles are:

- **Freestanding.** Typical freestanding models are 30, 36, or 40 inches wide. Both sides are finished.
- **High-Low.** A second oven, regular or microwave, on top provides extra capacity.
- **Drop-In.** Drop-ins look the most built-in but leave dead space beneath. They are usually 30 inches wide.
- **Slide-In.** The sides are not finished. Most are 30 inches wide; compact units are 20 or 21 inches wide.

Gas or Electric? Whether you choose gas or electric with which to cook depends in part on what's available locally. If natural gas is not available, appliance dealers can convert ranges to run on bottled liquid propane—but you'll need to arrange for regular delivery.

Many accomplished chefs prefer to cook with gas because gas burners heat up fast, cool quickly, and can be infinitely adjusted to keep food simmering almost indefinitely. Electric cooktops, on the other hand, are easier to clean. Also, new developments in cooktops, such as magnetic-induction cooking and smooth-top surfaces, are designed for electricity, not gas. Although many people prefer gas for surface cooking, ovens are a different story. Electric ovens maintain more even temperatures than gas units. So, many people choose a dual-fuel unit that combines a gas cooktop with an electric oven.

Restaurant-style ranges look similar to commercial appliances but without the ventilation and clearance drawbacks.

Restaurant-Style Ranges

True restaurant, or commercial-quality, ranges with heavy-duty burners deliver more heat more quickly than the usual kitchen range, and their ovens have superior insulation. Commercial-type cooking surfaces are made of cast iron, making them ideal for prolonged, low-intensity cooking. The sturdy appearance of a restaurant range appeals to serious cooks.

However, restaurant ranges are for restaurants. The tremendous heat that they generate will increase the risk of fire and injury in your home. Codes for installing this type of range are strict—some areas even prohibit the installation of commercial equipment for residential use. A commercial range also requires special venting and minimum clearances between it and adjacent cabinets or other combustible materials or surfaces.

As an option, you may want to consider a commercial-style range. They look like those used in restaurants, but more importantly they produce less heat—though more than standard ranges. They allow you to set flames as high as 15,000 Btu—30 to 50 percent higher than regular residential ranges—and to bring them down to 360 Btu (on some models) for low simmering. Some units come with the option of one high-flame burner (12,000 to 15,000 Btu).

Cooktops

A surface cooking unit has top burners only and fits into the countertop. Be sure the counter fabricator knows you will be installing a cooktop. Most of the space underneath can be used for conventional storage.

Gas. Usually 30 or 36 inches wide, gas cooktops have brushed-chrome or porcelain-enamel finishes. If you think gas cooktops are difficult to keep clean, new sealed gas burners may be the answer, because the cooking surface is extended around the heating element. No more drip plates or escaping flames.

Electric. Conventional electric cooktops have coil or cast-iron disk burners. Disks heat more evenly than coils and are easier to clean.

Ceramic Glass. Also called a radiant-heat cooking surface, a ceramic top features electric coils directly under translucent glass, which transfers heat more efficiently to the cookware than do older, opaque, white ceramic surfaces. It also uses higher-wattage heating elements. The smooth, sleek appearance of ceramic glass cooktops appeals to contemporary tastes. The finish is scratch- and stain-resistant, but it can be damaged by abrasive cleansers. You'll need flat-bottomed, heavy-gauge metal pans to heat food quickly and effectively with ceramic glass.

Halogen. Similar to ceramic glass cooktops, especially with regard to cookware and cleaning, halogen units combine resistant heating wires and halogen lamps that are located beneath a ceramic-glass cover to create heat.

Induction. This ceramic-glass cooking surface uses electromagnetic energy to heat the cookware, not the cooktop, making it safe because no heat is generated by a flame or coil. An induction cooktop is also easy to keep clean because the surface remains relatively cool, and spills don't burn and turn into a crusty mess that requires scrubbing.

Below the surface, the coils produce a high-frequency alternating magnetic field that flows through the cookware. Most of the heat from the cooktop is absorbed by the pan. Without a pan or utensil, the heating coil is de-energized and turns itself off. Induction cooktops require magnetic-responsive cookware, which means pots and pans for use with this appliance must be steel, porcelain-on-steel, stainless steel, or cast iron. Manufacturers of induction cooktops boast of its quick response—it can go from high heat to low heat instantly—and the precise temperature control.

Gas cooktops, top, provide the precise temperature control many cooks desire. Ceramic glass cooktops, bottom, have smooth, easy-to-clean surfaces.

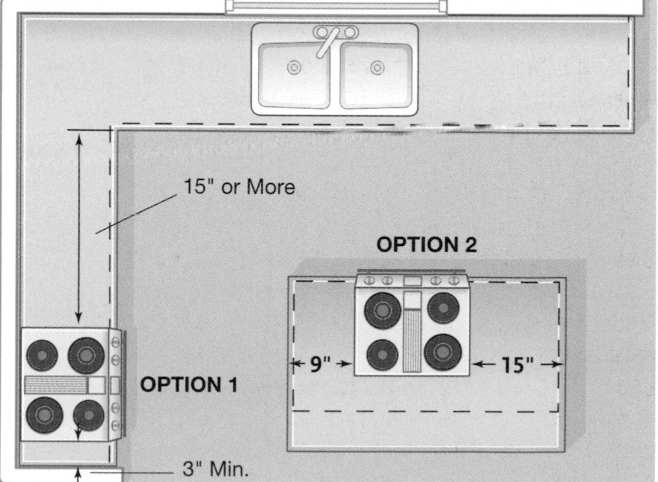

Plan adequate counter space near cooktops and ranges. Provide heat-proof surfaces in these areas.

5 Appliances

Removing an Old Dishwasher

If you're replacing a worn-out dishwasher, you'll need to remove the old unit before you can install a new machine. Start the job by turning off the power to the appliance at the electrical service panel. Then protect the floor in front of the old unit so it won't be damaged as you work. If you have prefinished wood flooring like the type shown here, generally you can pull out the old machine without any damage. But if you have vinyl sheet flooring, which is much softer than wood, place some cardboard over the floor and slide the unit onto it.

Tools & Materials

- Screwdriver
- Nut driver
- Adjustable wrench
- Bowl or pan

1 The first step in taking out an old dishwasher is to remove the access panel below the main door. Look for a couple of screws on both ends of the panel that, when removed, will free it from machine's framework.

2 Once the access panel is removed, loosen the nut that holds the water supply tubing to the machine using an adjustable wrench. Place a bowl under the tube to catch any water that may drain out. Also remove the electrical cable.

3 Once the water and power connections are removed, the only things holding the machine are two screws driven into the underside of the countertop. These are located at the upper corners of the unit. Remove the screws, and pull the unit out by holding onto the door.

Built-In Dishwasher

What if your kitchen wasn't designed with a built-in dishwasher in mind? With custom cabinets, it's going to be tough to create an opening. But if your kitchen has stock cabinets, with standard-sized units screwed together to make a continuous run, it's possible to remove one of the base units to make room for a dishwasher.

A conventional dishwasher requires a cabinet opening 24 inches wide, 24 inches deep, and at least 34½ inches tall, as measured to the underside of the countertop's edge band. (Most companies also make compact 18-inch models, which fit 18-inch-wide cabinet spaces.) The target cabinet should be a door unit. A drawer unit would work, but most kitchens have too few drawers for convenient storage already.

In conventional installations the dishwasher sits next to the sink cabinet, but this is not the only possibility. If you need to, you can skip a cabinet's width, but don't place the dishwasher more than 6 feet from the drain outlet. Not only will it be a hassle moving dishes from the sink to the dishwasher, but the unit's purge pump may not be up to the distance. If you do skip a cabinet's width, drill the side walls of the intervening cabinet, and pipe the water and discharge tubes straight through, tight against the back wall.

To free a cabinet, you'll have to remove three sets of screws, plus the toekick trim. One set of screws joins the cabinet stiles (the vertical hardwood framework). If you don't find them in the target cabinet, look at the stiles in the adjoining cabinets. The next set of screws will be in the corner brackets at the inside top of the cabinet. These secure the countertop to the cabinet. The final few will be in the back brace. These secure the cabinet to the wall studs. Toekick trim can be made of wood, hardboard, or vinyl. Work it loose using a pry bar.

Installing a New Dishwasher

Most appliances come in a few standard sizes so they will fit in typical kitchen layouts. If you are replacing an old dishwasher, you are practically ensured that a new one will fit in the space. Just make sure to measure the existing machine, and take these measurements with you when you shop for a new unit. All dishwashers come with adjustable feet. So if you have a tight fit, you can lower the feet to slightly reduce the dishwasher's overall height. Make sure to adjust all four feet the same amount.

Tools & Materials

- Dishwasher, fittings
- Nut-and screw-drive
- Needle-nose pliers
- Wire connectors
- Wire strippers
- Adjustable wrench
- Pipe sealing tape

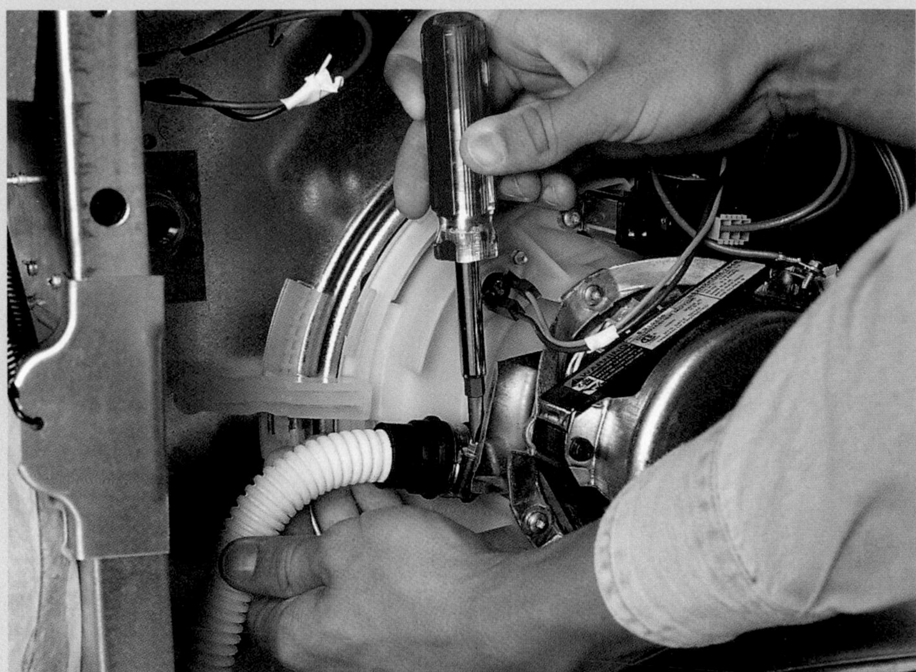

1 Before you slide the unit into its opening, attach the discharge hose that comes with the unit to the dishwasher pump. Use the hose clamp or the grip ring that's supplied for this purpose. This hose carries the waste water to the house drain system, usually through the side of the disposal unit.

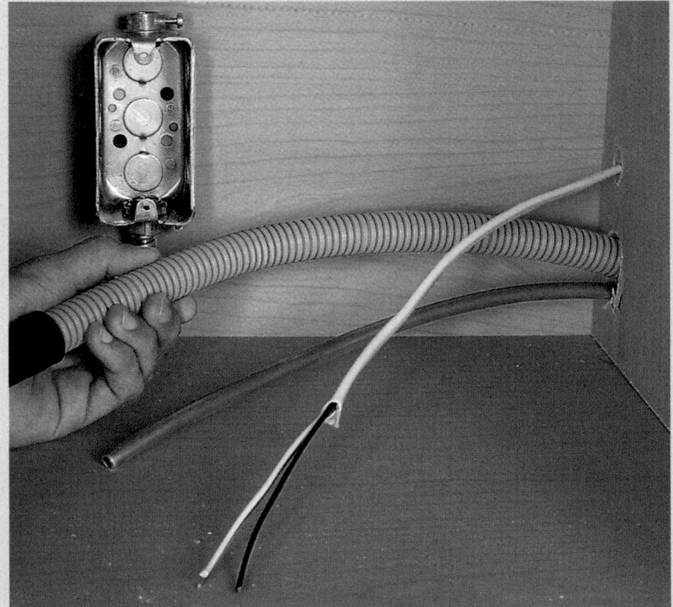

4 Some local building codes require a direct hookup from the dishwasher to the service panel. Others require a switch in the adjacent sink cabinet so that the power can be turned off easily. For the latter, install a switch box, and drill holes for the drain hose, water line, and electrical cable.

5 Remove the existing hot-water supply valve from under the sink, and install a new dual-stop valve. This fitting has a compression opening on the top for the sink supply tube and one on the side for the dishwasher supply tube. Install the fitting so that the side port faces the dishwasher.

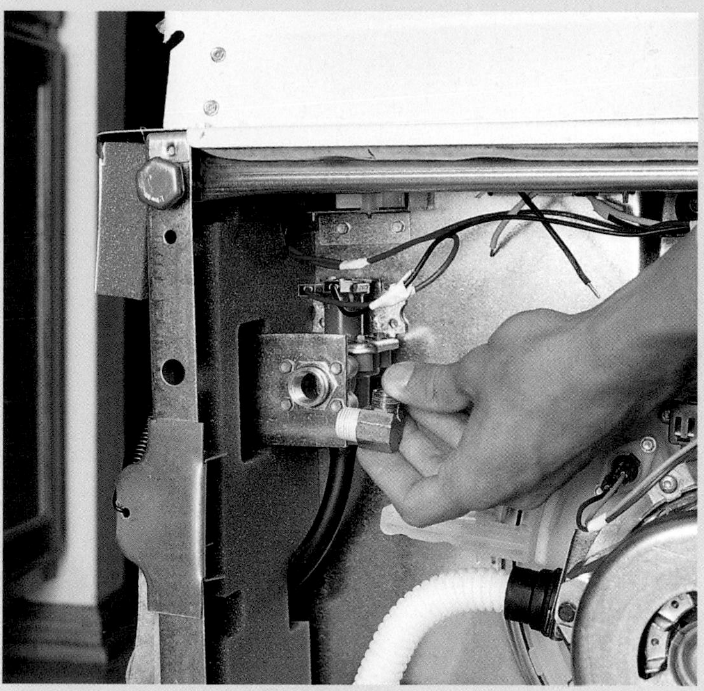

2 The solenoid valve is the entry point for the water supply line. It's designed to receive a standard dishwasher elbow; a fitting with pipe threads on one end and compression threads on the other. Wrap pipe-thread sealing tape around the pipe threads, and install the elbow.

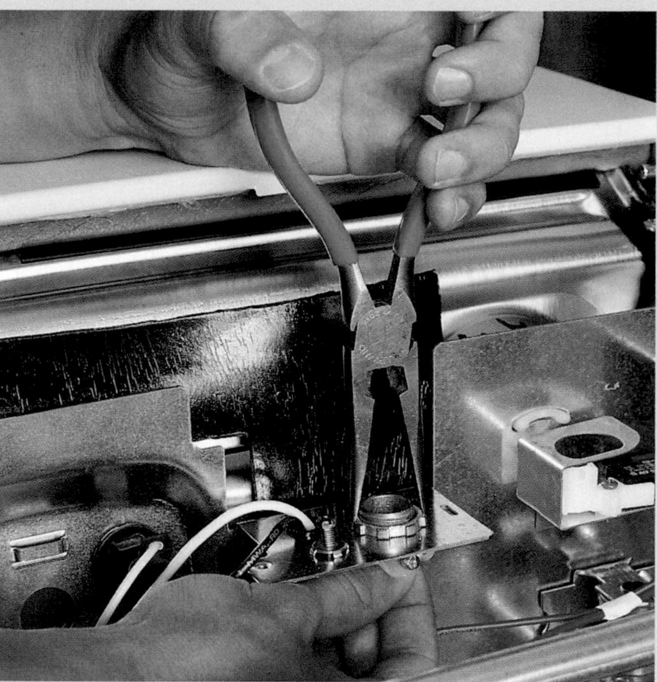

3 The electrical cable that brings power to the appliance must be installed in the electrical box that's provided. Remove the knockout plate on the side of the box, and install a cable connector. Wait to install the cable until after the unit is pushed into place.

6 Slide the dishwasher into its cabinet opening slowly to avoid scratching the floor and to keep from damaging the electrical cable, drain hose, and water supply tube. Have a helper pull these into the sink cabinet as you push the machine into place.

7 Once you have pushed the dishwasher completely into its place, turn down the leveling legs at the front of the machine using an adjustable wrench. Make sure that the unit is level from side to side when you are done.

Continued on next page.

Installing a New Dishwasher (continued)

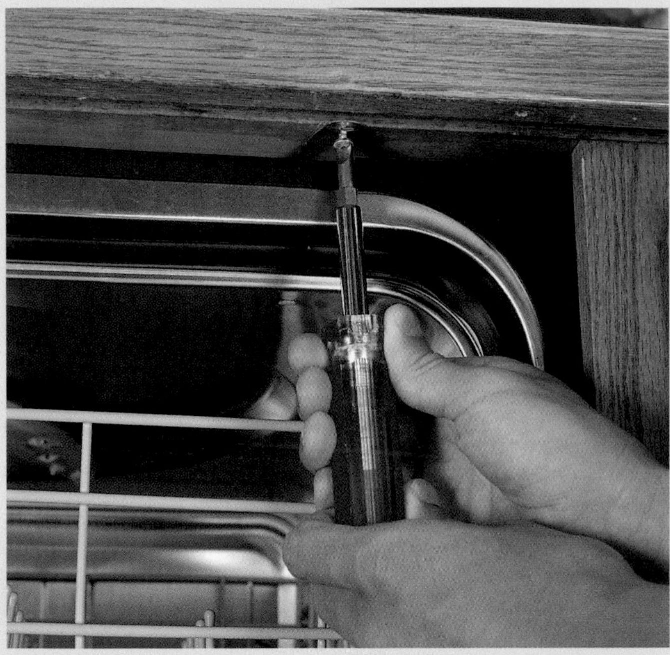

8 Dishwashers usually have two fastening brackets located at the upper corners of the machine. These are accessible only when the door is open. They are designed to be screwed to the underside of the countertop. Drilling screw pilot holes will make driving the screws much easier.

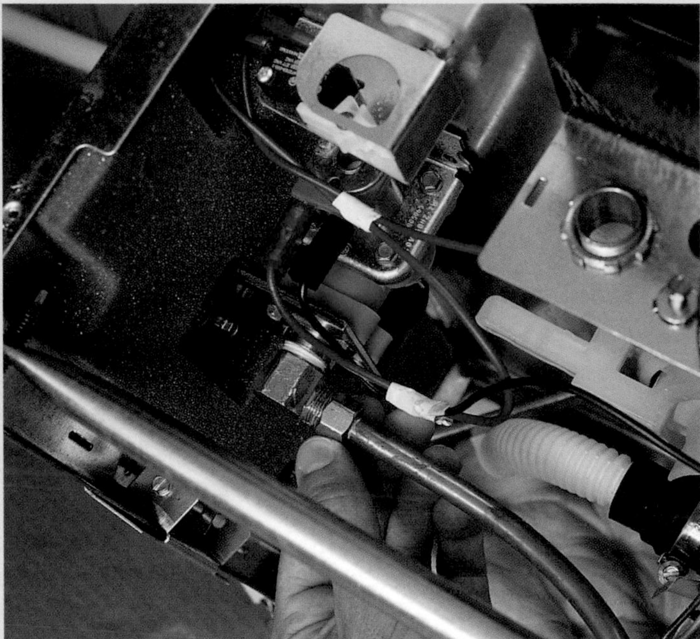

9 Water is delivered to the solenoid valve with ⅜-in.-diameter flexible copper tubing. Hook this tubing in place with a compression ferrule and nut. Tighten the nut securely with an adjustable wrench, but don't overtighten. This can ruin the ferrule.

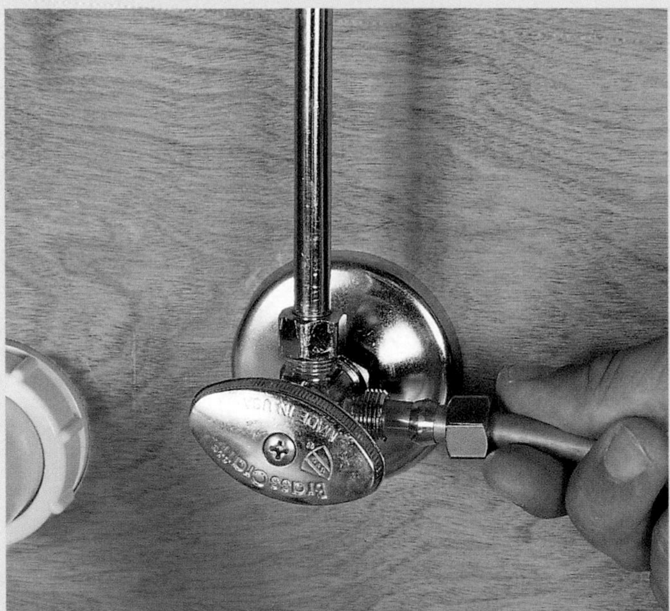

12 Install the sink supply tube to the top of the hot-water valve and the dishwasher supply tube to the side port. Carefully tighten the compression nuts so they are snug but not so tight that the ferrules are deformed. Once the water is tuned on, check for leaks and tighten if necessary.

13 Plumbing codes require overflow protection for the drain hose. This keeps the overflow from a backed-up drain from entering the dishwasher. The best way to do this is to install an air gap. You can also loop the hose to the top of the cabinet, and secure it with a piece of pipe strapping.

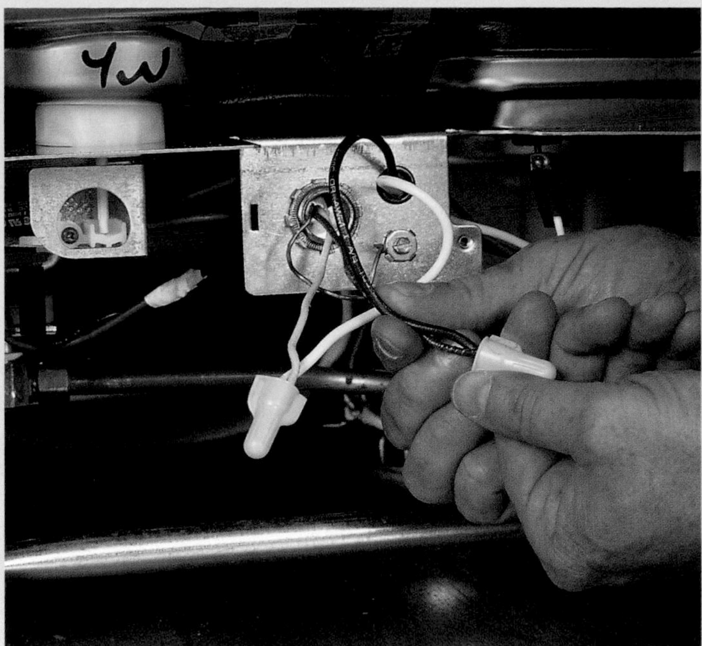

10 Insert the electrical cable into the electrical box, and tighten the cable connector screws. Then strip the sheathing and paper from the cable and about ⅝ in. of insulation from each wire. Join the cable wires to the dishwasher wires using wire connectors.

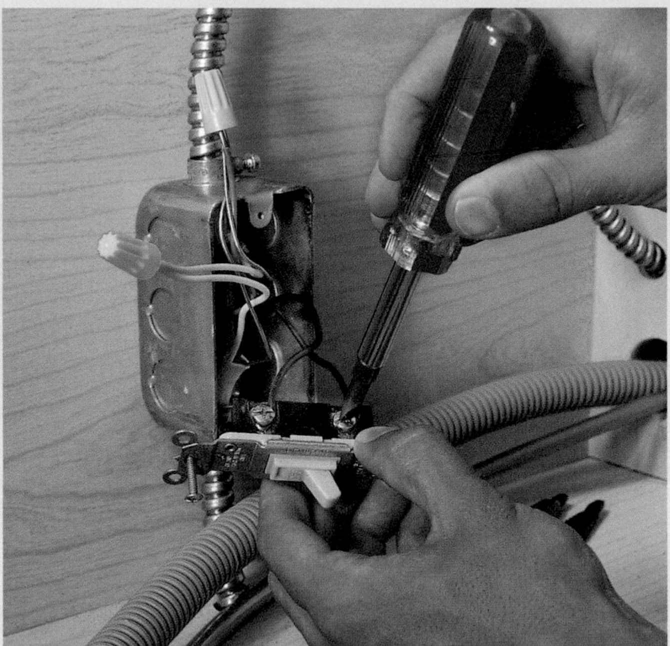

11 Slide the cables into the switch box, and tighten the box connectors. Strip the sheathing from the cables and insulation from the ends of the wires. Join the white wires with a wire connector; attach the ground wire to the box; and screw the black wires to the side of the switch.

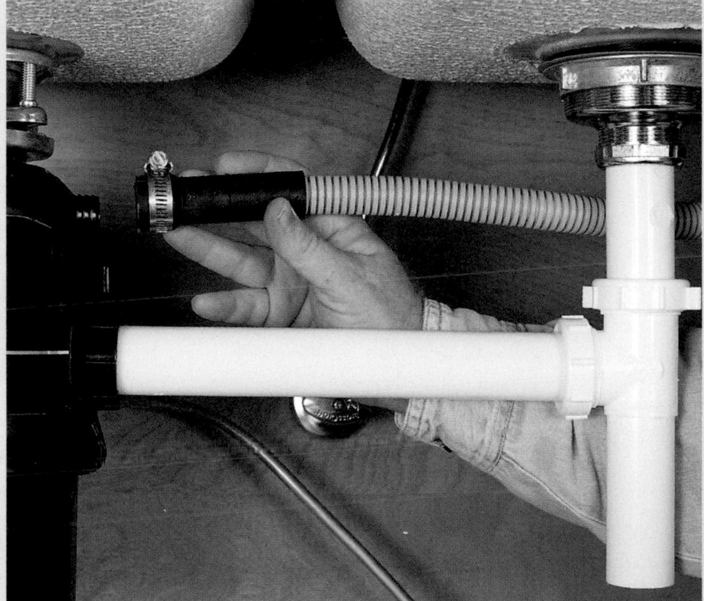

14 Waste-disposal units have a built-in side port for hooking up the discharge hose from a dishwasher. To use this port, first break out its plug with a screwdriver, then push the end of the hose over the ribbed nipple. Attach the hose by tightening the hose clamp with a screwdriver or nut driver.

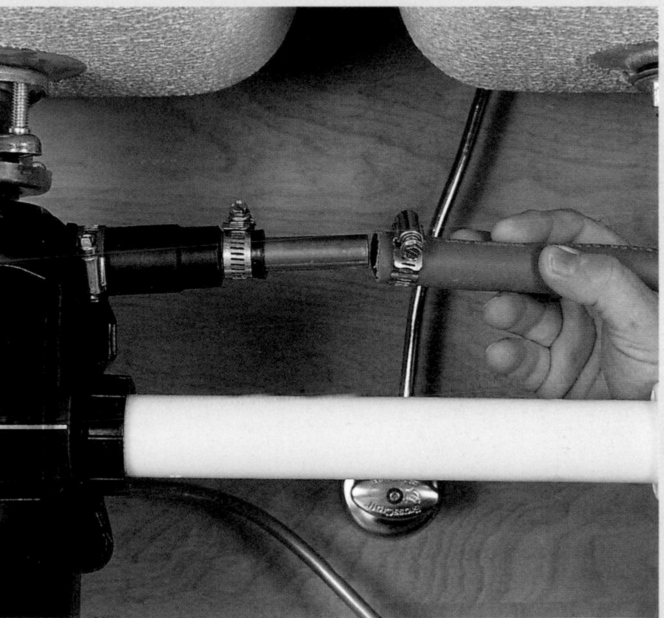

15 If the discharge hose is made of standard heater hose, you need a rubber adapter and a short length of copper pipe to make the connection. Check requirements in your area.

Installing a Water Filter in a Sink Cabinet

Water-treatment systems come in many different varieties. The best one for you depends on what's in your water. So your first step is to have your water tested. There are simple do-it-yourself test kits available, but you'll get a more-thorough analysis if you send the sample to a testing lab. Once you get your results back, shop for a filter that will remove the impurities in your water.

Tools & Materials

- Filtration system
- Installation kit (saddle valve, water lines with compression fittings if not included with the system)
- Screwdriver
- Adjustable wrench or appropriate open-end wrenches
- Pliers

1 The carbon filter unit is designed to mount under the kitchen sink. Clear a space near the cold-water supply pipe, and mount the canister on the side of the cabinet. Some units simply hang on a couple of screws, like this one. Others are installed on a simple bracket.

2 If your sink has a knockout plug for a sprayer or hot-water dispenser, this is the perfect spot for the filter faucet. Just remove the knockout using a flat-blade screwdriver. If you don't have a hole, you can drill one through the sink or the countertop next to the sink to provide easy access.

3 Lower the filter faucet into the hole; then tighten it in place by installing a mounting nut from below the sink. Have someone above hold the faucet so that it points in the preferred direction while you tighten it from below.

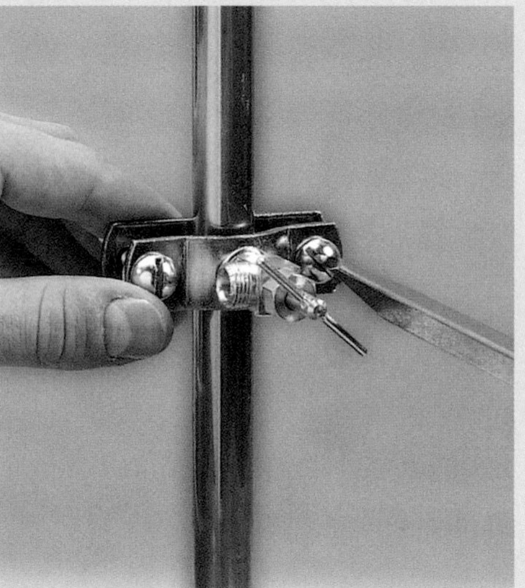

4 Make the water connection to the cold-water pipe using a simple saddle valve that comes with the filter kit. Back out the tapping pin on the valve; then hold the plates against the pipe, and alternately tighten the bolts a little at a time until the assembly is tight. Turn the tapping pin clockwise until it pierces the pipe.

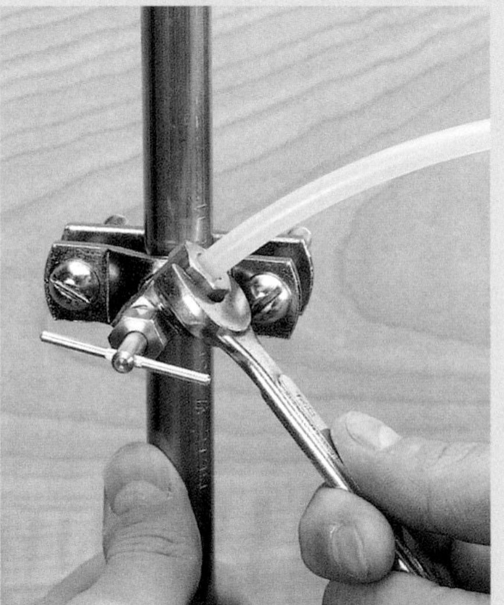

5 Join the filter unit to the saddle valve with a plastic hose and a compression fitting. Then run hose between the filter and the faucet, again using compression fittings. Turn on the water supply, and check the installation for any leaks. If you find any, try tightening the compression nuts.

Installing an Electric Cooktop

Installing a cooktop is very much like installing a typical kitchen sink. You just trace a template on the countertop, cut an opening, and lower the appliance into the hole. Most cooktops are held in place by simple clips that are screwed to the underside of the countertop. It's usually a good idea to run some silicone caulk under the rim to provide the best seal.

Tools & Materials

- Cooktop
- Junction box
- Electrical cable
- Wire connectors
- Tape measure
- Template
- Saber saw
- Power drill-driver
- Drill bits

CAUTION

Check with your local building inspector before attempting this type of installation. The latest version of the National Electric Code states that if the circuit is new, the appliance must be wired hot to hot, neutral to neutral, and ground to ground. The wiring shown here is wiring for an existing circuit.

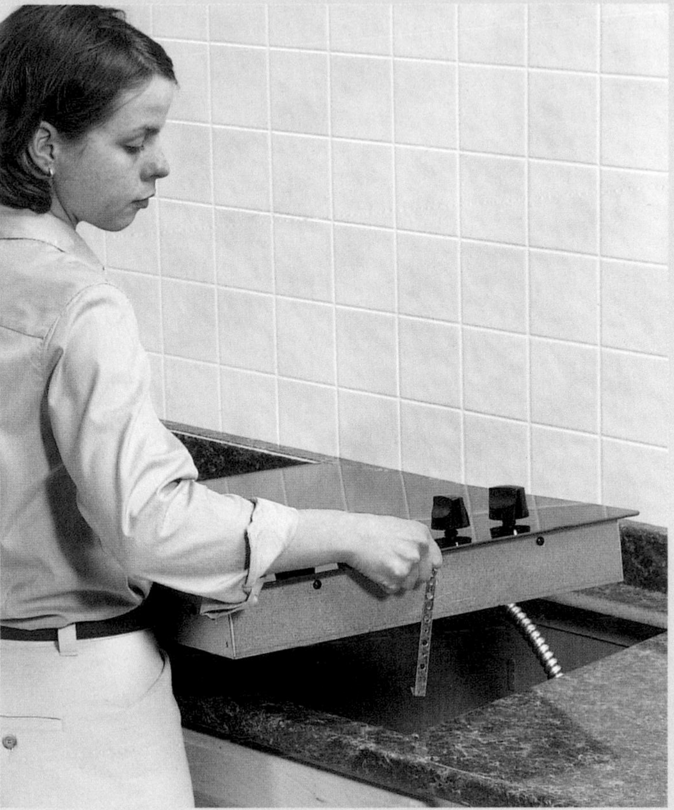

1 Place the cooktop template on the countertop according to the manufacturer's instructions. Then trace the template, and cut the hole with a saber saw. Test-fit the cooktop by lowering it into the opening. When satisfied, remove it; apply silicone caulk to the bottom of the rim; and put the cooktop back in the opening.

2 Once you have aligned the cooktop properly in the countertop cutout, move inside the cabinet and attach the mounting clips from below. Use an electric or cordless drill-driver and short screws.

3 If you're replacing an old cooktop with a new one, the electrical connections are easy. Just bring the new cable from the appliance into the existing electrical box, and tighten the cable clamp. Then join the red wires together and the black wires together using wire connectors. Finish up by joining the white and ground wires.

Installing a Range Hood

The hardest part of installing a range hood is installing the duct work between the hood and the outside of your house. If the range is located on an outside wall, the best choice is to run the duct from the back of the hood straight through the wall. If the range is on an interior wall, the preferred route is usually from the top of the hood through the roof or a roof soffit. No matter where it ends up, the exhaust duct has to be covered with a duct cap, soffit grille, or roof cap.

Tools & Materials

- Range hood
- Electrical cable
- Basic carpentry tools
- Sheet-metal screws
- Duct tape
- Metal duct sized to fit unit

1 The cutout in the back wall of the cabinet connects to ducts that are installed inside the wall. Install the ducts before installing the new cabinets. To install the hood, cut a duct hole in the bottom of the cabinet using a saber saw. Also drill a hole for the electrical cable that supplies power to the unit.

Ducting Options

If the duct comes out through the side wall of the house, install a duct cap. Make sure that you seal around the perimeter of the cap with exterior caulk. If the duct goes through a soffit, you'll need a transition fitting to connect the round duct to the square grille.

2 With the circuit power turned off and the hood resting on the range, pull the power cable into the hood and tighten it with a cable clamp. Then join like-colored wires with wire connectors, and attach the ground wires to the green grounding screw.

3 Attach the hood to the underside of the wall cabinet using screws. It's a good idea to also drive a couple of screws through the two sides of the hood and into the adjacent cabinets. Have a helper hold the hood while you work.

4 Connect the duct at the top of the hood to the duct inside the wall. Two 45-deg. adjustable elbows will usually do the job. Once the parts fit together properly, join the elbows to the ducts and each other using sheet-metal screws and duct tape.

5 If the duct passes through the roof, you need to install a weatherproof duct cap. To do this, cut an opening in the shingles that matches the size of the cap. Then slide the cap over the duct and under the shingles. Hold it in place by applying plastic roof cement over the cap flange and under the roof shingles.

chapter 6

bathroom cabinets

The Vanity and Other Cabinetry

Like fixtures and fittings, a vanity can make an important statement about how the new space will look, as well as how it will function. A vanity brings style into a bathroom while providing an area for grooming and storing toiletries and other sundries. Today there are numerous creative ways to approach the vanity. It can be a custom design or a stock piece. Look at kitchen cabinets, too. Some of these cabinets, such as pantry units, are interchangeable with bathroom storage pieces. Style-wise, you might be surprised by the sophistication offered by some manufacturers, even in the budget category.

Just as in the kitchen, cabinetry in the bathroom now features fine-furniture detailing. A variety of designs and finishes suits many decors, from modern to traditional. Inside, optional organizing systems make better use of storage space, allowing you to keep grooming and cleaning products handy and neat. A mirror and a medicine cabinet to match or coordinate with a vanity cabinet are optional.

Whether you shop for a vanity and other cabinetry or plan to build them to your specifications, give it as much consideration as you would cabinetry for the kitchen. Top-of-the-line solid-wood construction may be too expensive for most budgets; however, a sturdy plywood frame combined with dovetail and mortise-and-tenon joinery is excellent. If you buy stock cabinets, make sure that the interior is well finished and the shelves and drawers are not flimsy.

As when selecting kitchen cabinets, estimate your storage needs before buying bath cabinetry. The bath above contains plenty of storage options.

Adapting furniture designed for other rooms is a popular option. Tops should be waterproof, and the insides must accommodate plumbing.

Mirror space is just as important as counter space in the bathroom. This vanity not only provides a full-width mirror but also includes both drawer and cabinet storage.

Installing a New Vanity

If you want a truly custom vanity cabinet and have experience in cabinetmaking, consider designing and making your own (which is beyond the scope of this chapter). If you'd prefer to keep it simple, however, check out the selection of prefabricated units available from your building-supply or kitchen-and-bath store. Prefab units usually have post-formed tops: particleboard that's been factory-laminated and often includes a built-in backsplash. All vanities come as base-only units, a base with an integral sink-countertop, or a base with a countertop for a separate sink. The steps shown here describe how to install a prefab vanity cabinet with a post-formed countertop, complete with backsplash. (See page 88 for instructions on installing a new sink into a laminated or post-formed countertop.)

Tools & Materials

- Vanity unit
- Power drill-driver
- Saber saw
- Level
- Shims
- Wood plane
- 2½-inch wood screws
- Countertop
- Straightedge
- Clamps
- Wood glue or construction adhesive
- Masking tape
- Paint or sealer
- 1¼-inch wood screws
- Silicone caulk and caulking gun

CAUTION

Installing a vanity isn't a hard job. The only real problem is hooking up the water supply lines so that they are leak free. Otherwise, your new vanity can sustain quite a bit of damage in just a few weeks. Test the connections after you turn on the water. And check them again in a couple of days to make sure they are still dry.

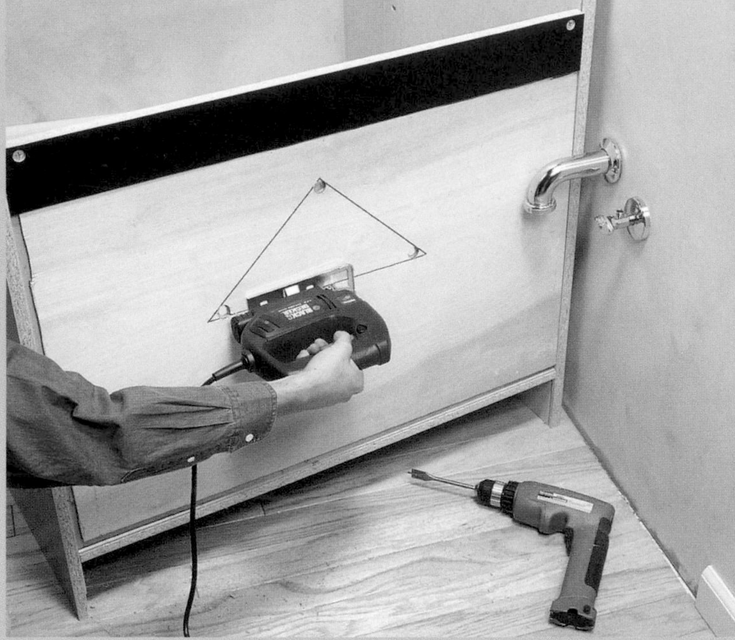

1 Locate the proper place for the vanity; then mark a triangle on the back of the cabinet to provide clearance for the supply and waste lines. Drill blade-entry holes at all three corners, and cut out the waste using a saber saw.

4 Stock countertops usually have to be cut to length to fit a vanity. Do this job with a saber or circular saw. For best results, cut from the underside of the countertop, clamping a metal straightedge in place to act as a guide.

2 Push the vanity against the wall, and check it for level from front-to-back and side-to-side. Slide wood shims under the low points to lift up the cabinet. If a section is too high, scribe it to the floor; then trim off the extra stock using a circular saw or a hand plane.

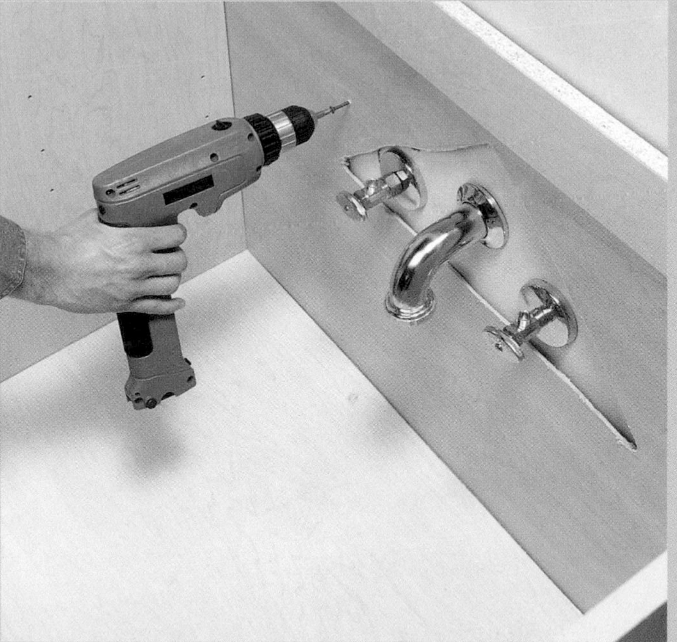

3 Attach the vanity to the wall by driving screws through the back of the cabinet into the wall studs. Wall studs almost always fall on 16 in. centers. So once you find one stud, measure 16 in. along the wall to find another.

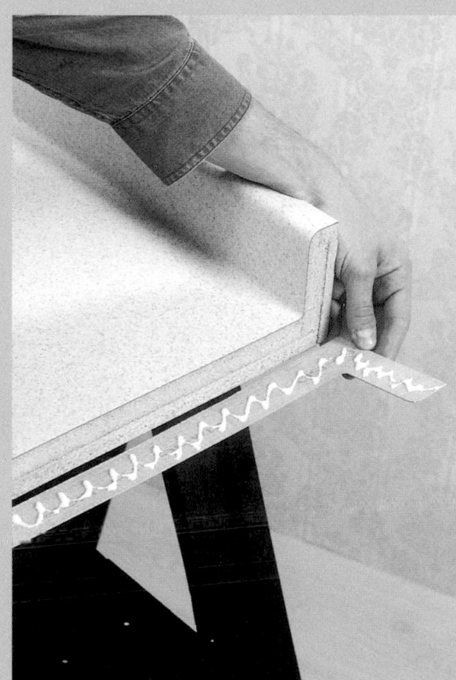

5 Once the top is cut to length, the ends need to be covered with end-cap pieces. Use wood glue to attach these strips, and hold them until dry with masking tape.

6 Place the counter on top of the vanity cabinet, and push it tight against the wall. Attach it by driving screws from underneath up into the bottom of the top.

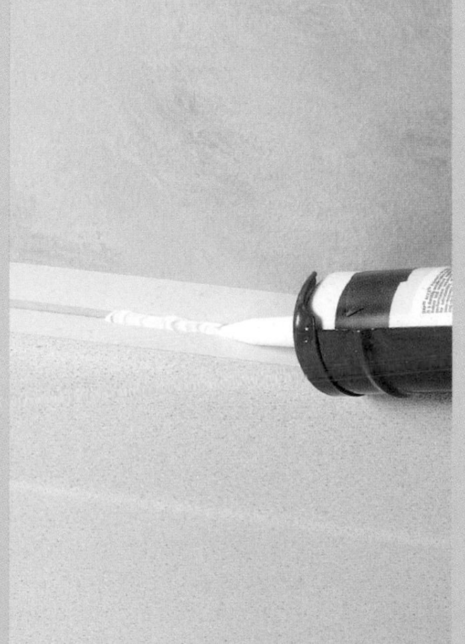

7 The last installation step is to caulk the joint between the top of the backsplash and the wall. Use silicone caulk for best results.

Installing a Medicine Cabinet

A medicine cabinet is a great place to store the odds and ends that clutter our bathrooms. But the standard 14-inch-wide cabinet, designed to fit between wall studs, doesn't hold very much. This is why so many people are adding either bigger medicine cabinets or separate cabinets elsewhere in the room. Because space is almost always a premium in bathrooms, both types of cabinets are designed to be recessed into the wall. This makes very good use of space but complicates the job. You'll have to cut out one or more studs to make the cabinet fit. We show this process for a partition wall that doesn't carry any structural weight. If your wall is load-bearing, like an outside wall or a wall that supports ceiling joists, the opening needs to be reinforced, which is a job best left to a carpenter.

Tools & Materials

- Magnetic stud finder
- 4-foot level
- Power drill-driver with screwdriver bit and ¾-inch spade bit
- Utility or keyhole saw
- Backsaw
- Wood plane
- Rasp
- 2x4s
- 3d, 6d, 8d, and 10d (1¼-inch to 3-inch) nails
- Drywall taping knife
- Sandpaper
- Paintbrush
- Drywall
- Drywall tape
- Joint compound
- Paint
- Cabinet
- Screws or nails for cabinet
- 3½-inch-long L-clips

Hidden Wires and Pipes

Every bathroom wall has a good chance of hiding wires and pipes. The only good way for most of us to find where they are is to open up the wall. Drill access holes, and cut drywall carefully to avoid damaging these materials.

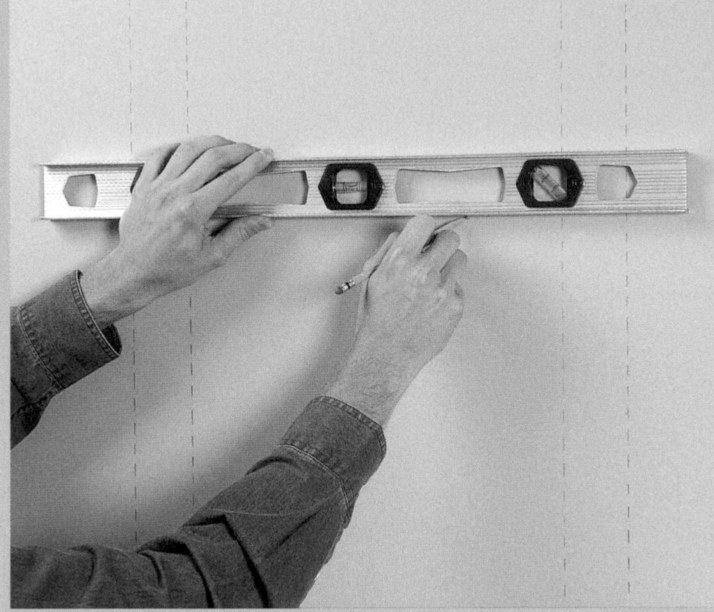

1 Determine the side-to-side location of the cabinet; then measure up from the floor 72 in. to mark the height of the cabinet. Using a level as a guide, mark a level cut line for the top of the cabinet on the wall.

4 Frame the opening using 2x4 blocks cut to fit between the studs. Nail these blocks directly into the cut studs, and toenail them into the uncut studs on both sides. If the cabinet is smaller than the opening, close down the opening with a trimmer stud nailed to small blocks on the sill and the header framing (inset).

2 Draw the outline of the cabinet on the wall; then add $1\frac{1}{2}$ in. to the top and the bottom of the outline for new framing. Next, drill an access hole at each corner, and carefully cut the drywall between the holes using a keyhole saw. If you hit anything, put the saw aside and use a utility knife to cut the drywall.

3 Once you have removed the drywall, the wall framing will be exposed and you will be able to see how many studs have to be cut for the cabinet to fit. In this case, only one stud needs cutting. To make the cuts, use a backsaw or a reciprocating saw.

5 Nail drywall pieces to the part of the wall that won't be covered by the cabinet. Then finish all the seams using paper tape and joint compound.

6 When the joint compound is dry, sand it smooth using 120-grit sandpaper. Remove the dust, and apply a coat of primer. Then paint the patch to match the rest of the wall.

7 Slide the cabinet into the opening, and attach it to the surrounding framing with screws. Make sure the cabinet is square and level before driving the screws.

Sinks

Sinks are often called lavatories or basins by the industry. But if it looks like a sink and works like a sink, it probably is one. Sinks come as ovals, rectangles, circles, and other shapes. Manufacturers have gone to great lengths to give sinks appeal by sculpting their forms, but the simpler shapes are both more practical to use and easier to keep clean. Sizes vary from a 12 x 18-inch rectangle to a 33-inch-diameter oval.

Sinks used to be made of either glazed vitreous china or porcelain. These sinks' finishes proved impervious to water, mold, and mildew; they dulled only after years of abrasion. Modern innovations in fiberglass, acrylic, metal, and glass open endless possibilities for shapes, colors, and patterns, but they are much more susceptible to scratches. Fortunately, manufacturers have created many cleaning and maintenance products to keep these sinks looking like new.

Integral Sinks

One-piece sink/countertop units are molded from a single material, such as solid-surfacing material or faux stone. There are no seams with this kind of sink. The look is seamless, sleek, and sculptural. Many of these units contain preformed backsplashes, built-in soap dishes, and other useful design features.

Self-rimming sinks are easy to install and work well with most countertop materials.

Freestanding Sinks

A good place to begin your sink selection is to decide whether you want a freestanding fixture or one built into a countertop. Freestanding sinks—including those designed specifically to go into corners—can be mounted either directly on the wall or on legs or pedestals. Freestanding sinks are available in colors, shapes, and sizes to suit any taste. They come with flat tops or raised backsplashes that meet the wall. If you choose a freestanding sink, be sure to allow enough space in your design. Wall-mounted units will look and feel cramped if they abut a wall or other fixture with minimal clearance at the sides. While you can stuff a pedestal sink into a space as narrow as 22 inches, it will look better with generous open space on each side. Also keep in mind that you're losing under-sink storage with a freestanding sink, which may affect the rest of your bathroom layout.

Freestanding and pedestal sinks come in both traditional and modern designs.

Vanity-Mounted Sinks

Vanity-mounted sinks became popular when bathrooms shrank to the tiny size that marked much of the housing built after World War II. For extra storage, the space under the fixture was enclosed in a cabinet; any extra space above could be used to hold accessories such as drinking glasses, toothpaste, or soap. Combination vanities and sinks may not be much wider than the sink, or they may be as wide as the room. If you are stuck with a bathroom measuring 50 square feet or less, a vanity-mounted sink may be the only way to get enough storage space.

Sinks mounted on a countertop are self-rimming (where the bowl forms its own seal) or rimmed (where the bowl is installed with a metal trim piece to join it to the countertop). Under-mounted sinks are installed from below, creating a sleek look; however, the edges of the countertop must be able to withstand moisture. Molded solid-surface countertops, stone, and ceramic tile work well for this kind of application. However, plastic laminate, which has a seam at the edge, will not hold up.

The way the sink is mounted in the countertop has both aesthetic and practical consequences. The exposed edge of a self-rimming sink sits atop the vanity surface. Though attractive, the edge prevents water splashed onto the counter from draining into the sink. Metal rims overcome this drawback by aligning the edge of the sink with the countertop, but the metal trim usually creates a less-elegant look than the self-rimming model. Sinks mounted below tile, solid-surfacing material, or stone countertops provide a pleasing separation between countertop and sink.

Create drama by choosing an unusual installation method, such as this cantilevered design.

Above-counter sinks are available in a variety of materials, including metal.

Undermounted sinks look best with solid-surfacing or stone countertops.

Installing a Sink in a Laminate Vanity Top

Most bathroom sinks are either self-rimming or metal-rimmed models. The basic difference between the two is how each is attached to the vanity top. Self-rimming units rest on top of the counter and are kept from moving by metal clips that are installed from underneath or by a generous bead of adhesive caulk. Metal-rimmed units, on the other hand, are attached to the underside of a metal rim, and the metal rim is attached to the counter. The drawings below show the difference between the two.

These days the self-rimming type is more common. It is the type installed here. In many contemporary bathrooms, the sink of choice is more often an above-counter model (see opposite page), which works as well as the other sinks, but has a much more distinctive look.

Tools & Materials

- Sink and laminate countertop
- Power drill-driver with ⅜-inch bit
- 2x4s for bracing
- 8d finishing nails
- Colored wood filler
- Hammer
- Nail set
- Saber saw
- Adjustable wrench
- Screwdriver
- Utility knife
- Silicone caulk and caulking gun

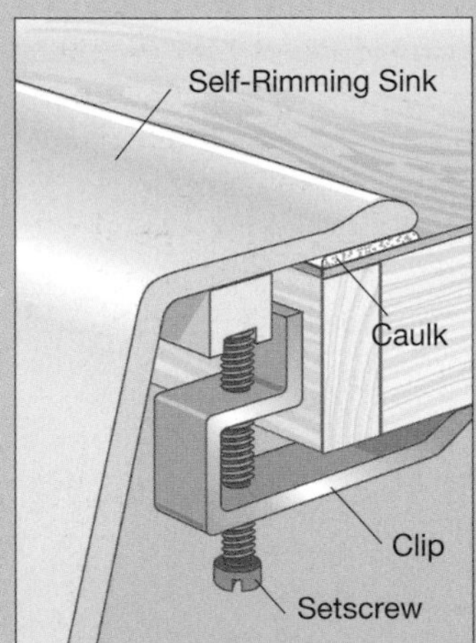

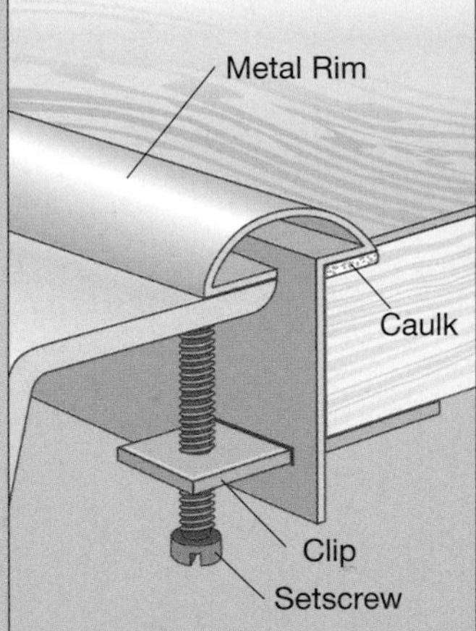

Self-rimming sinks are set in caulk and held with clips. Rimmed sinks, on the other hand, are supported by metal rims that are set in sealant. The sink is pushed up against the rim from below and is held by a clip.

1 Mark the centerline of the sink location on the vanity top. Then mark the centerline of the sink on the underside of its rim. Turn the sink over, and place it on the countertop so that the two marks line up. Then trace around the perimeter of the sink.

4 Cut the sink opening using a saber saw. Make sure that you use a sharp blade and hold the saw firmly against the vanity top. If the saw bounces up and down when you are cutting, this can mar the surface. If you can't keep the base from bouncing, cover it with duct tape to prevent any damage.

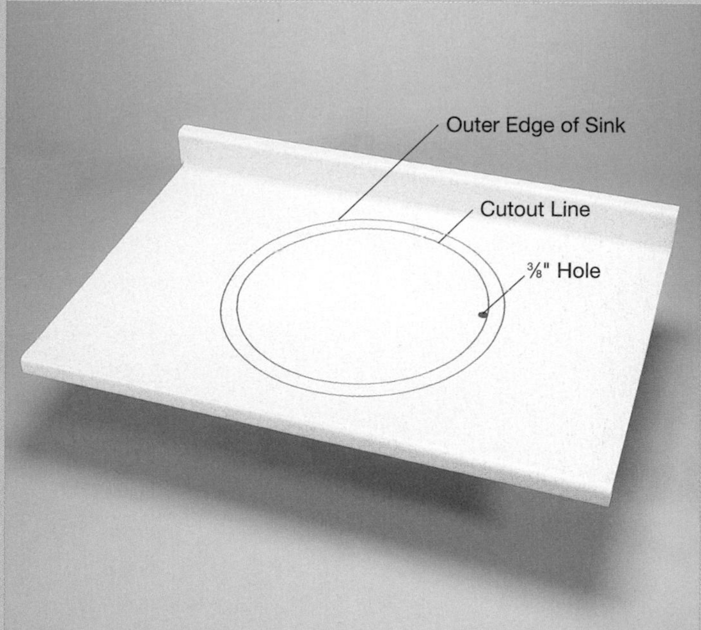

2 Consult the installation instructions that came with your sink to establish how far inside the traced line the cut line should fall. Mark this cut line; then drill a blade-entry hole through the countertop on the inside edge of the cut line.

3 Provide extra support for a heavy sink by installing a 2x4 brace on both sides on the sink opening. Attach them with screws driven through the cabinet framing and into the ends of the braces. On the finished side of the cabinet, use finishing nails; set their heads; and fill the holes with colored wood filler.

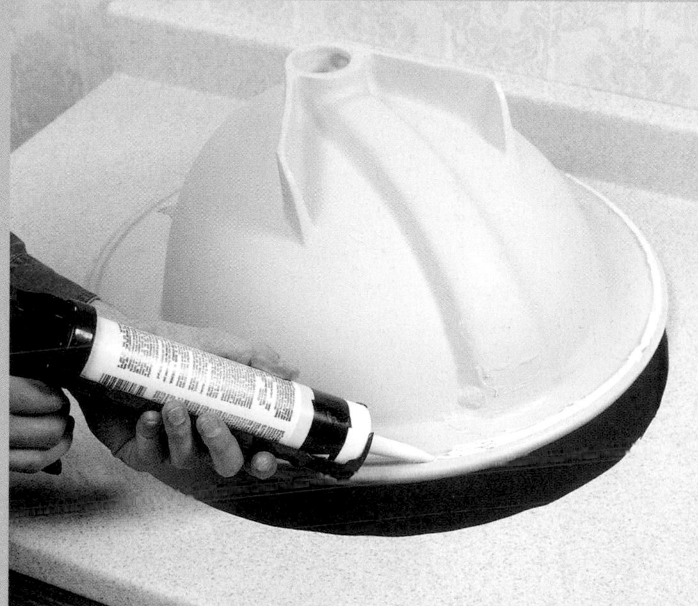

5 Before putting a self-rimming sink into the opening, apply a generous bead of silicone caulk to the underside of the sink rim. Then turn the sink over, and lower it into place. If the sink needs clips, install them now. Let the caulk dry, and clean up any caulk squeeze-out.

Above-Counter Sinks

For an arresting—and easily installed—addition to your bathroom, consider an above-counter, sometimes called a vessel, sink. An above-counter sink is one step beyond a self-rimming sink—it's designed to sit on top of the counter rather than down inside it. A sink intended as a vessel sink must have finished surfaces both inside and out. These sinks are available in cast iron, ceramic, and even translucent glass. They are plumbed in the same way as any sink, but remember that your faucet must be tall enough to curve over the top of the sink's edge.

Installing a One-Piece Faucet

Bathroom faucets are pretty simple. Most are one-piece devices with either two separate handles for hot and cold water or a single handle, much like a typical kitchen faucet. They either have flexible copper supply tubes (photo 2) or standard tailpieces (photo 3). We show installing a faucet in a freestanding sink, but installing one in a countertop requires the same process.

Tools & Materials

- Adjustable wrench
- Tubing bender (optional)
- Clean rag
- Silicone caulk & caulking gun
- New faucet
- Braided stainless-steel risers (if chromed copper supply tubing not included with faucet)

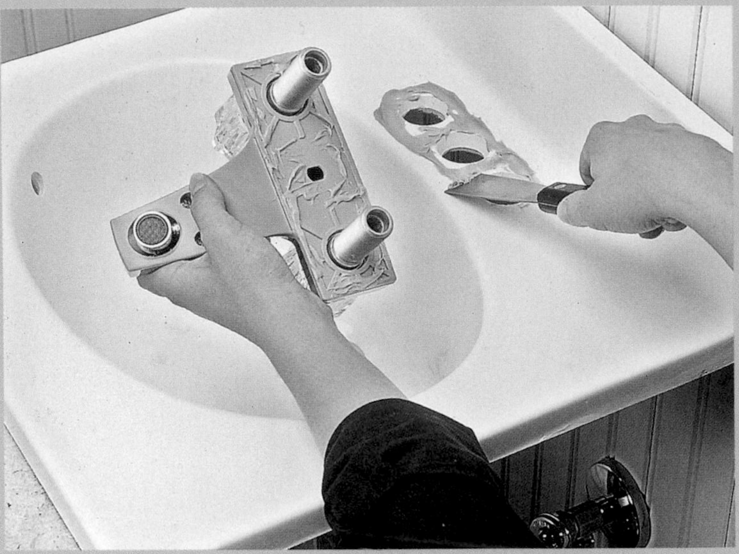

1 If you are replacing an existing faucet, take off the old faucet by removing the water supply lines and unthreading the mounting nuts on the faucet tailpieces. Then slide a putty knife between the faucet and the sink and gently pry off the faucet. Clean any remaining caulk from the sink or counter.

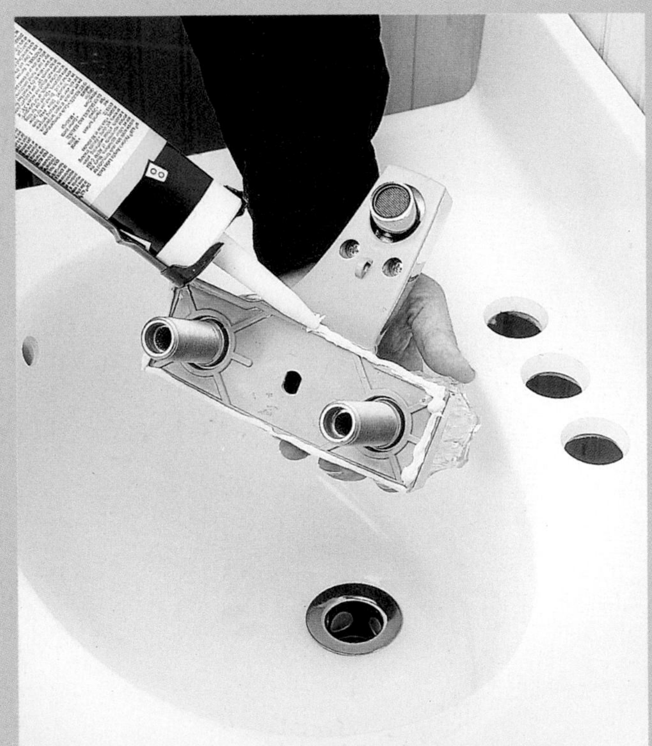

3 On faucets that don't have a gasket, run a bead of silicone caulk or plumber's putty around the perimeter of the base. Then press the faucet into the sink holes, and let the caulk or putty dry. Cut away any excess caulk or putty that squeezed out around the base using a sharp utility knife.

4 If the new faucet has pre-attached copper supply tubes, it won't have threaded tailpieces. Instead the faucet will have two threaded bolts that get fitted with washers and nuts. To secure the faucet, just tighten the nuts on these bolts using an adjustable wrench.

2 New faucets usually have a gasket that must be installed between the faucet and the sink to prevent water from leaking around the base of the unit. Put the gasket over the holes, and lower the faucet onto the gasket.

5 The best way to join the faucet's copper supply tubes to the shutoff valves on the wall is to use braided stainless-steel risers. Use an adjustable wrench to tighten both of the compression fittings on each riser.

Bending Tubing

If your faucet has flexible copper (or chromed copper) supply tubing pre-attached to it, you may need to bend the tubing slightly to reach from the faucet to the shutoff valve. To do this, you'll need to use a tubing bender, which looks like a pipe made from concentric rings. You just insert the flexible tubing into the sleeve, and bend it slowly into shape by hand. This tool will minimize the crimping that often occurs when you bend flexible tubing with only your hands.

Dual-Lever Faucet Setup

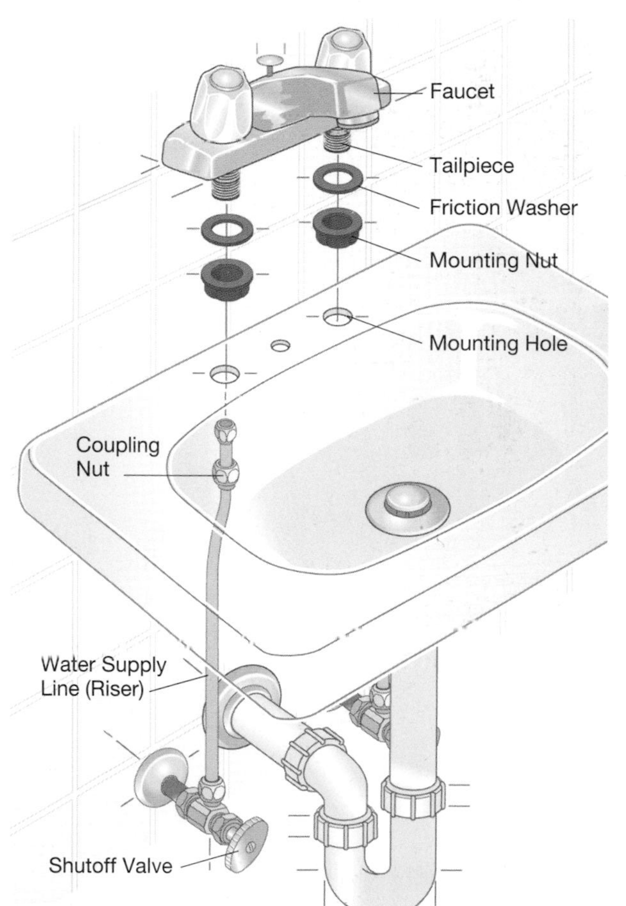

To begin disassembly, close the water shutoff valves in the hot- and cold-supply risers below the basin.

chapter 7

building cabinets

Construction Basics

If you have the time and inclination, building your own cabinets is a great way to make any room better. You can create them to fit the space you have instead of buying stock units that may not fit as well. You can also use exotic materials that aren't available at most cabinet retailers. Antique pine boards or rescued flooring from an old house can make wonderful, one-of-a-kind cabinets.

In this chapter you will find some basic cabinet-building techniques, including ways to reinforce joints using dowels; cutting dadoes and grooves, and rabbets using a table saw or router; building doors; and adding hinges and other hardware. You can use the techniques to complete the two projects shown in this chapter or use them to construct a cabinet of your own design.

The first project is a simple retrofit of an existing kitchen base cabinet. In no time at all, you can increase the functionality of the cabinet by installing a rollout shelf. The other project is a linen cabinet. It is a bit more involved, but once completed will provide valuable storage space for a variety of items. The cabinet is almost 7 feet tall with four doors. You can build the cabinet using a paintable material, such as poplar or pine lumber, but you can also substitute an attractive hardwood and then finish with a clear or stained finish.

Reinforcing Joints with Dowels

Wood dowels can increase the strength and improve the accuracy of butt joints. In face-frame construction, the joint usually includes two dowels glued into each end of a rail (the horizontal member) and then into corresponding holes in the stiles (the vertical members). Using a doweling jig helps ensure accurate results.

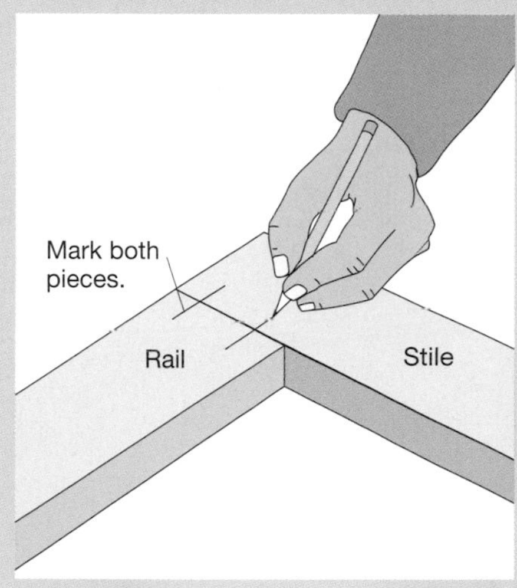

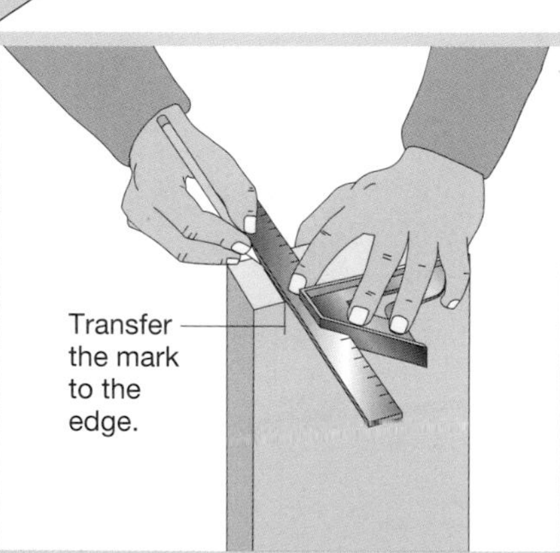

1 To start, you'll want to locate the dowel holes. To locate dowel holes accurately, temporarily position the two mating pieces in place. Strike a line on both members indicating the dowel locations. Transfer that mark onto the edge of each piece with a square.

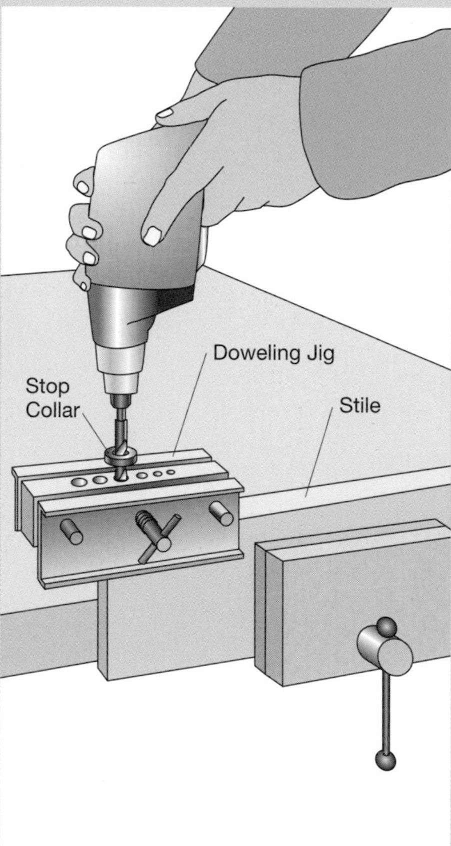

2 Drill the holes, use a doweling jig to ensure that the dowel holes are drilled exactly equidistant from the two faces of the piece. Use a stop collar or a piece of tape on the bit to indicate when you have drilled to the correct depth.

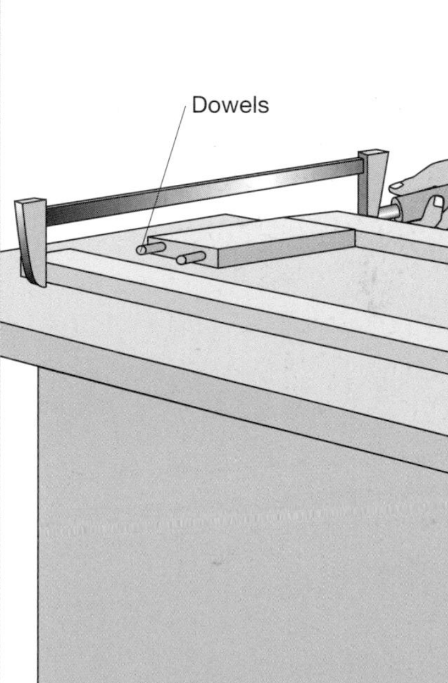

3 Assemble the parts by applying glue to the dowels and inserting them in the holes in one of the parts to be joined. Attach the mating part, and clamp the assembly until the glue has set.

Dadoes, Grooves, and Rabbets

Dadoes and grooves are identical except for their relationship in respect to the wood's grain: dadoes are actually a type of groove that runs across the grain; grooves that run with the grain are not dadoes. For the sake of clarity, we'll use the term groove to describe only grooves that run with the grain. A rabbet is like a ledge cut along one edge of a piece. Dadoes are commonly used for fitting shelves and partitions into cabinet panels. Grooves are commonly used for fitting partitions and insetting shelf standards, while rabbets most often are used for joining cabinet panels and insetting cabinet backs.

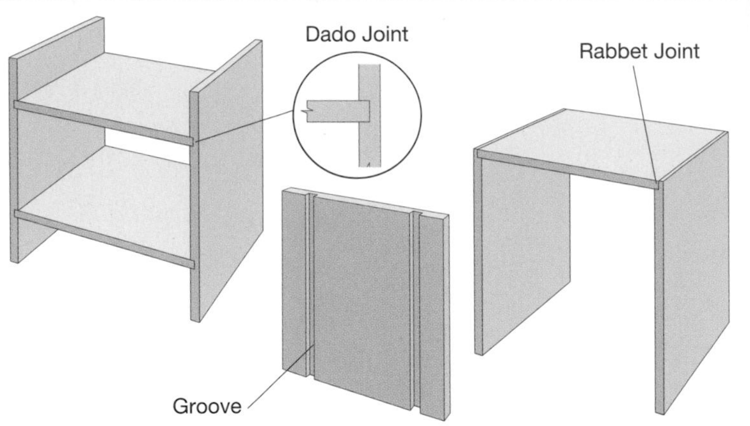

Making Dadoes and Grooves with a Table Saw

Use a rip fence when making dadoes and grooves on a table saw. This method is most suited to making long grooves. For example, this is a very handy setup for making grooves for insetting shelf standards.

Although you can use a table saw to make dadoes, the longer the panel is, the more awkward this operation will be. You will find that using a router is usually the better way to make dadoes in large cabinet sides.

Note: When working with a stacked or wobble-type dado blade, you may need a different throat plate with a wider opening than the one used with an ordinary blade. Install the dado head, and turn the blade by hand to test its clearance. If it makes contact with the throat plate, you will have to make a replacement wooden throat plate. Refer to your saw's owner's manual for instructions on installing a dado head.

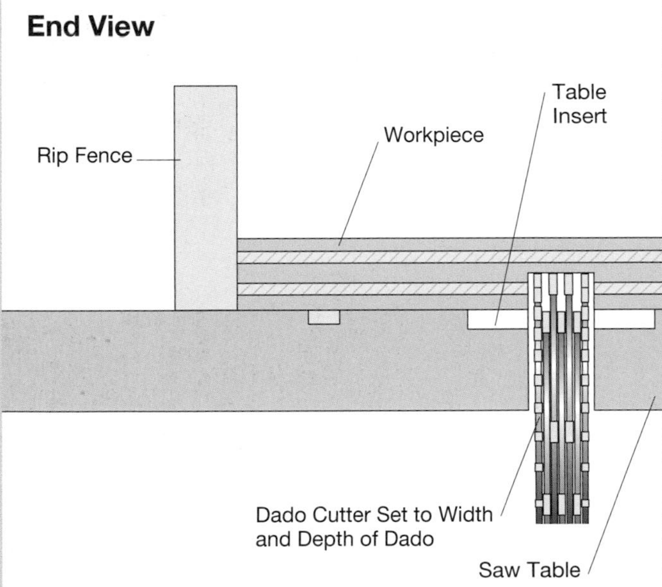

1 First, make a test cut. Unplug the saw, and replace your regular saw blade with a dado cutter. Use either the wobble-style or stacked cutter setup for the desired cut. Adjust the cutter for the proper depth of cut, and set the fence to the desired distance from the cutter.

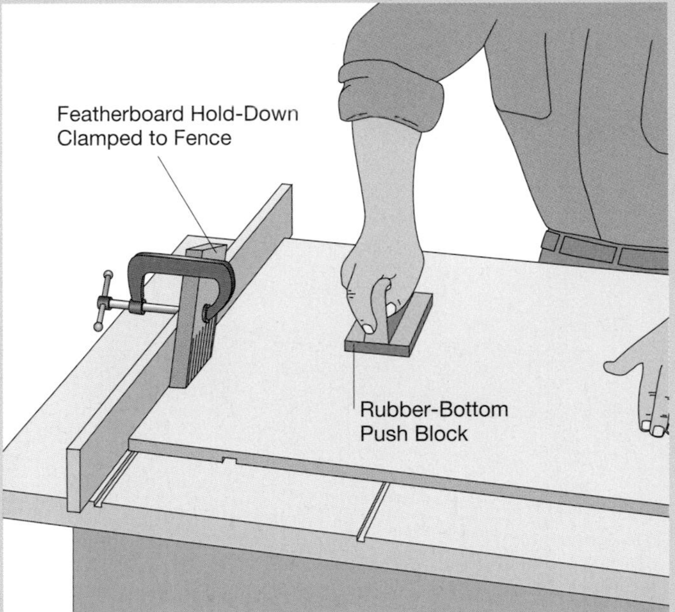

2 Now, make the final cut. To cut the groove or dado in your panel, simply run the panel over the blade, and make the cut. Always use push blocks and hold-downs where appropriate to keep the workpiece from lifting off the saw table or kicking back. You can make a featherboard hold-down simply by kerfing the end of a small board that has had its ends cut on the diagonal.

Making Rabbets with a Table Saw

Cutting rabbets on the table saw is similar to cutting grooves and dadoes, but you will need to equip your saw with an auxiliary wood fence made of ¾-inch plywood so that the blade can run right up against the edge. Again, because the rip fence is used, this operation is more suitable for cutting rabbets along the edges of long panels than it is for cutting rabbets along the top or bottom of long panels.

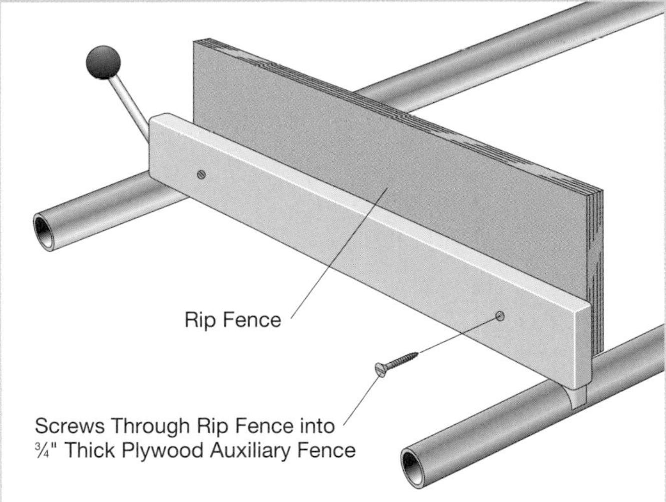

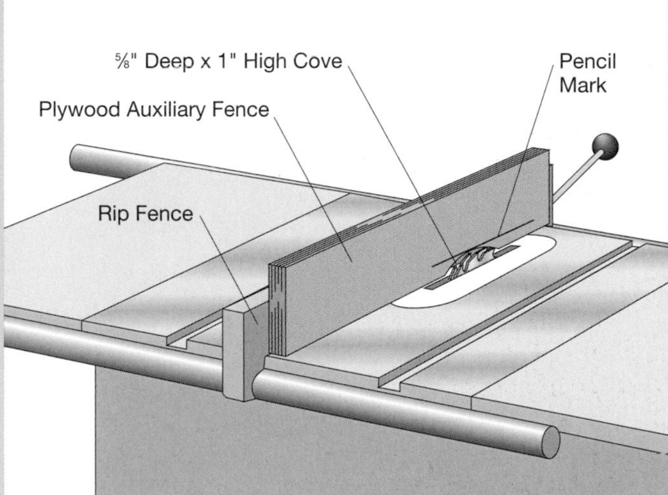

1 First, you'll want to make and mount the auxiliary fence. Make the auxiliary fence from ¾-in. plywood. Make the auxiliary fence the same length as the rip fence and a couple of inches higher than the rip fence. Screw the auxiliary fence onto your rip fence (refer to your owner's manual for specific directions). Install the cutter in your saw, and drop the blade below the saw-table surface.

2 To make the dado cutter easy to adjust, cut a blade cove into the auxiliary fence. With the dado cutter lowered beneath the saw's table, move the fence so that it extends over the blade by approximately ⅝ in., and lock it in place. Make a pencil mark on the left face of the auxiliary fence 1 inch above the saw table. Turn on the saw, and slowly raise the dado cutter until it hits the pencil mark.

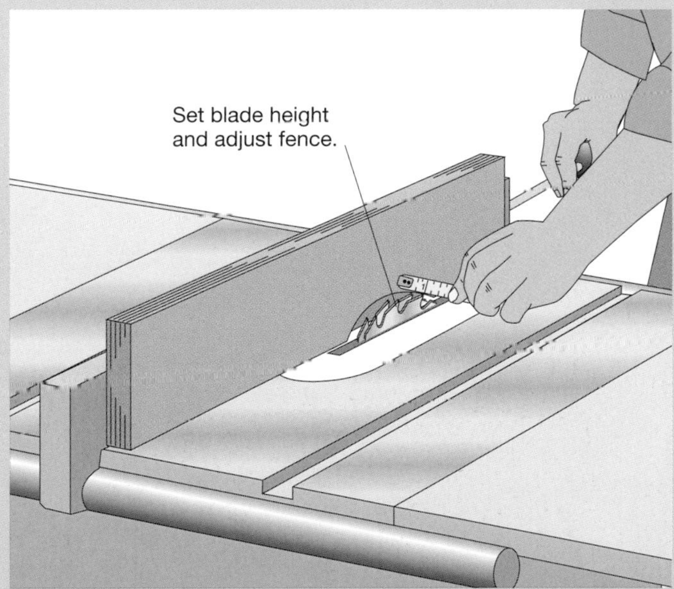

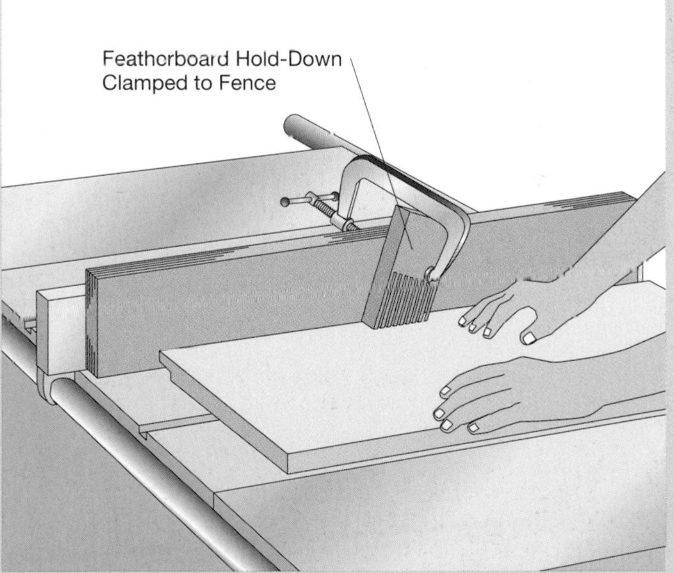

3 After mounting the correct dado cutter for your particular task to the saw arbor, set the cutter to the proper blade height and adjust the auxiliary fence to the desired rabbet width.

4 To make an accurate final cut, make a sample cut on a piece of scrap to check your measurements and saw settings. When the setting is perfect, put the workpiece on the table, and run the piece over the blade.

Making Dadoes with the Router

In cabinetmaking, if you are making a dado in a panel, chances are that you'll be making a matching dado in an opposing panel. The easiest way to make sure opposing dadoes are perfectly aligned is to cut them both in the same pass. You can do this by using a simple straight-edge as a guide, but you will find it is really worth your while to make a T-square router guide. When cutting dadoes with a router, it is very tricky to get the cutting edge of the bit exactly the right distance away from the straightedge guide. With the T-square guide, you cut a dado into the crosspiece, then simply align the dado to your layout line on the workpiece. The other advantage is, of course, that the T-square makes sure your dadoes are perfectly square to the edges of the workpiece. By routing one dado on each side of the crosspiece, you can use the guide for dadoes of two different widths.

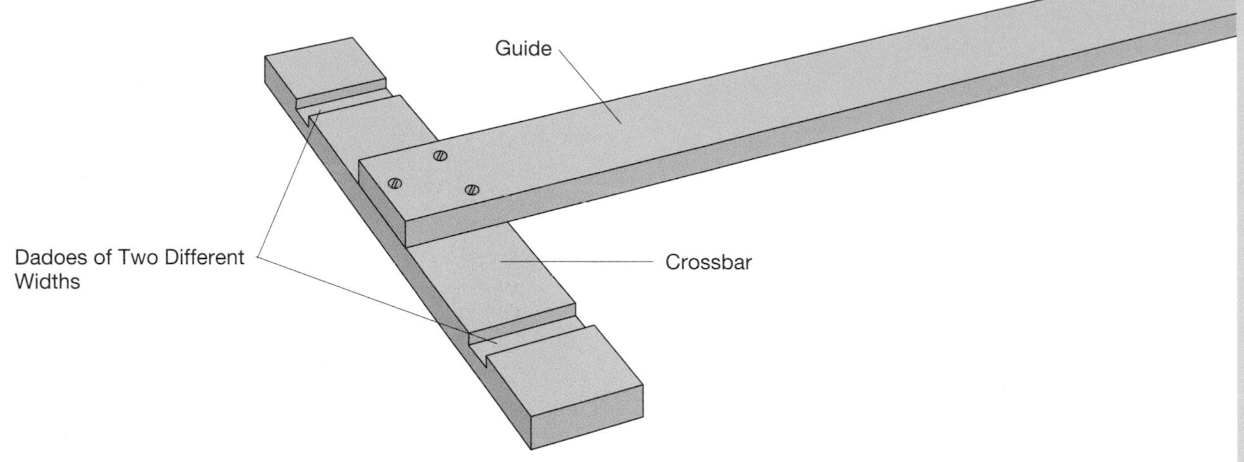

1 Construct the T-square guide from two pieces of ¾ -in.-thick plywood. Make the crossbar about 3 x 14 in. long. Make the guide 3 in. wide and about 3 in. longer than the width of your workbench. Assemble the guide using three screws positioned as shown in the illustration above. When the glue has dried, fit your router with a straight bit, the diameter of which matches the dado width you want to cut. Set the bit to the desired dado depth. Guiding the router against the guide, cut a dado in one side of the crossbar. Later, when you need a dado of a different width, you can make a cut in the other side of the crossbar.

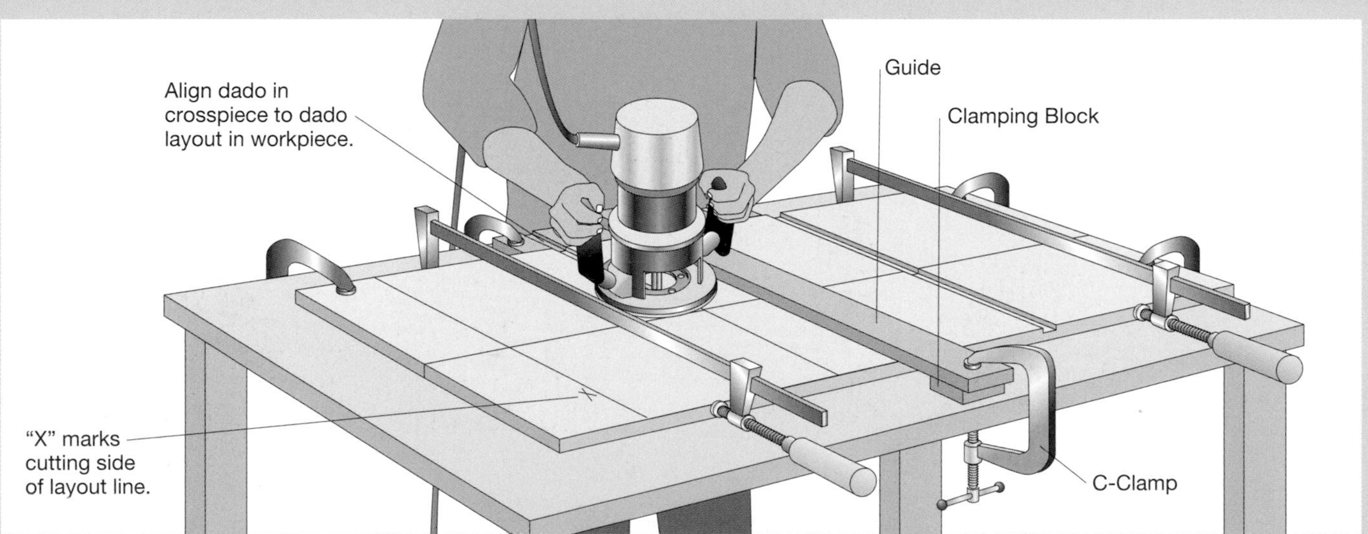

2 To use the cutting guide, align the dado in the crossbar to the dado layout on the workpiece. Clamp the work-piece to a stable work surface. Clamp both ends of the jig to the work surface. Or if the workpiece is narrower than the work surface, clamp one end of the guide to the work surface, and insert a clamping block that is the same thickness as the workpiece between the table and the other end of the jig, as shown. When using a router, work from left to right when the router is between you and the guide.

Making Rabbets with a Router

You can make rabbets using your router, a straight bit, and a straightedge guide. Another option is to purchase special bits specifically designed for cutting rabbets. The best rabbeting bits have ball-bearing tips that roll easily along the workpiece and prevent burning the edges of the wood. You can buy the bits in different sizes or in a kit that includes a carbide-tipped bit with interchangeable bearings for making rabbets of different dimensions.

Regardless of which technique you use, remember always to run the router through the stock against the rotation of the router bit. This will keep the bit from skating dangerously along the stock.

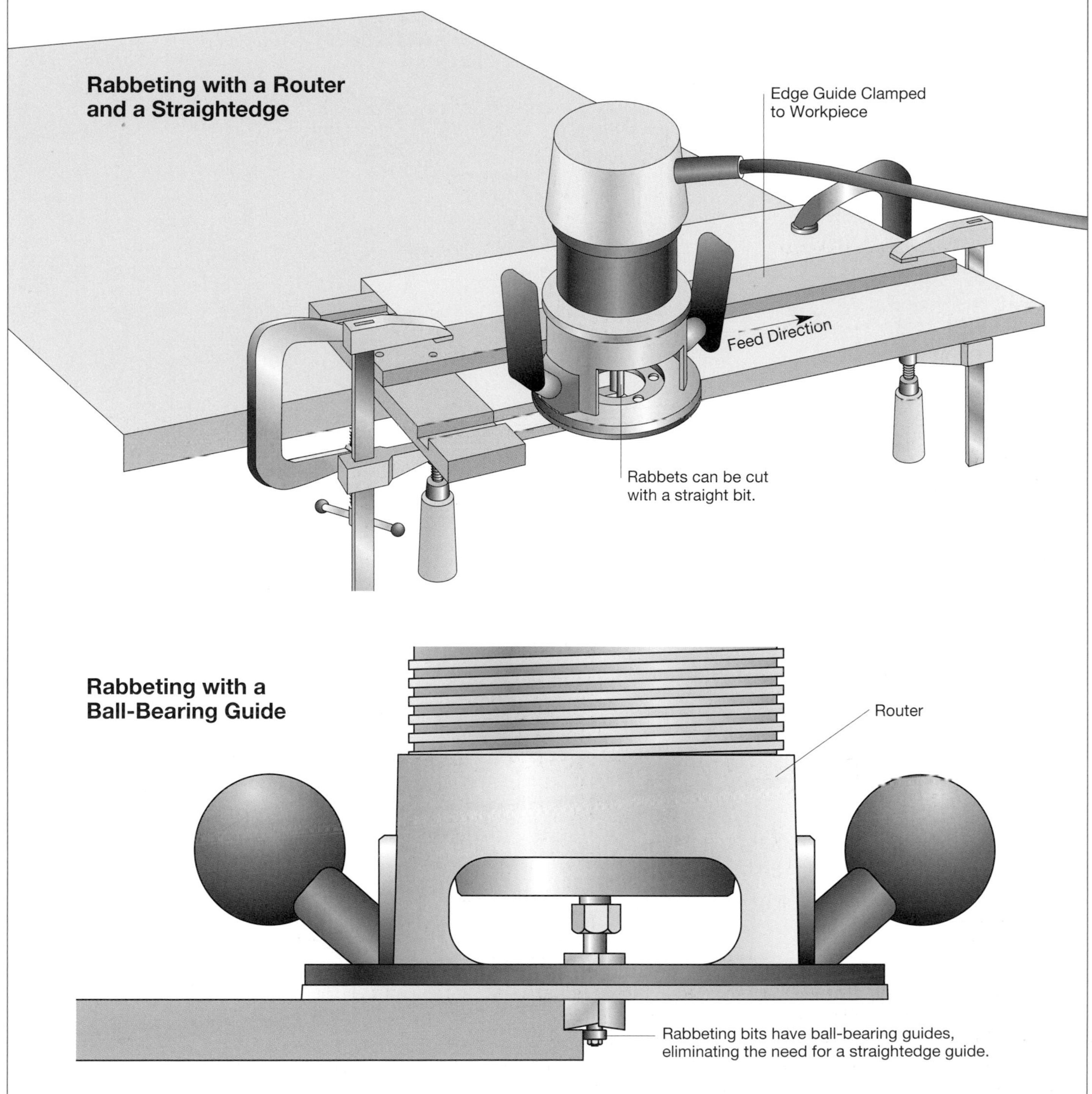

Rabbeting with a Router and a Straightedge
Edge Guide Clamped to Workpiece
Feed Direction
Rabbets can be cut with a straight bit.
Rabbeting with a Ball-Bearing Guide
Router
Rabbeting bits have ball-bearing guides, eliminating the need for a straightedge guide.

Squaring a Carcase

Working with plywood is beneficial in carcase construction because you can build a large carcase using just a few panels. However, carcase assembly can still be a real headache. Often, you are working with large, heavy panels, trying to position them exactly in place and keep them there long enough to drive a screw or until the glue has had enough time to adequately set the joint. Once they are in place, it is essential that the corners are perfectly square and that they stay this way.

Always check a carcase for square as soon as you have assembled it and before the glue has set. To check for square, measure diagonally from corner to corner. If the measurements match, the carcase is square.

If measurements don't match, you can reposition clamps or apply clamping pressure diagonally to bring the carcase into square before the glue sets.

Using the Back to Square a Carcase

It's possible to square up your cabinet accurately without ever reaching for a tape measure or framing square. As long as you maintain at least one corner of the back panel with a square corner (that is, the corner is made of two factory-cut edges), that will true up the rest of the carcase as you install it. The key to this procedure is to install the back immediately after assembling the carcase, while the glue is still wet and will allow you to shift things around a bit.

1 Install the back by applying glue to the back edges and dropping the back into position. Align the square corner with one top corner of your carcase, and secure it using an appropriate screw or finishing nail.

2 To align the carcase, shift the assembly so that it is flush along the bottom edge of the carcase, and drive one fastener through the bottom corner opposing the fastened top corner. Shift the whole assembly as necessary until the sides are aligned. Secure the remaining corners; then drive fasteners as necessary along the perimeter to clamp the back panel until the glue sets.

Squaring a Carcase

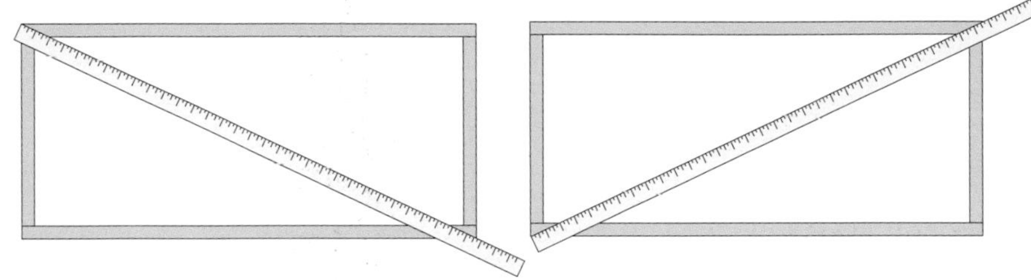

Measurements across both diagonals should be the same.

Using the Back to Square a Carcase

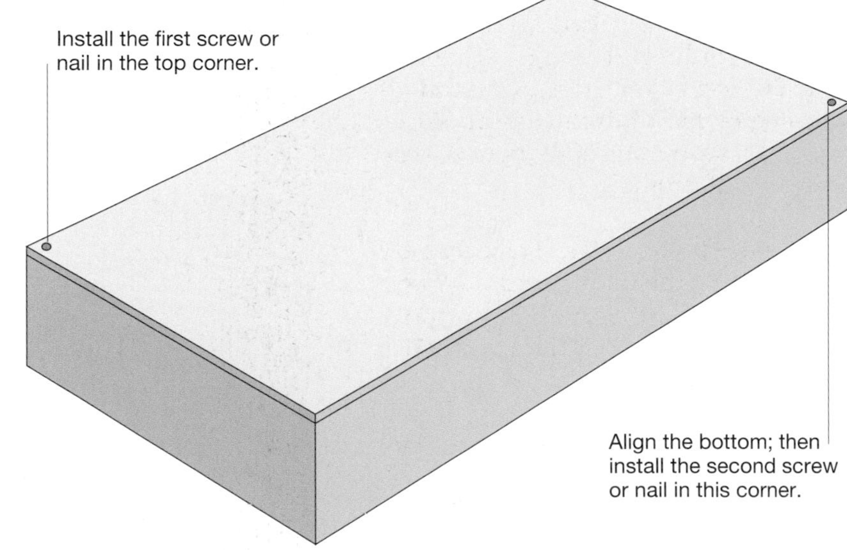
Install the first screw or nail in the top corner.
Align the bottom; then install the second screw or nail in this corner.

Building a Slab Door

This type of door can be as simple as a flat piece of wood or a panel of plywood, or it can be adorned with trim or faced with veneer for a more elegant effect.

1 Because slab doors are made of plywood, the exposed edges need to be covered with ¼-inch-thick strips of solid wood. So begin by cutting plywood panels that are ½ inch narrower and shorter than the final width and length you need.

2 Next, you'll want to cut the edge strips by ripping each strip out of the same wood species as the face veneer of the plywood. This way, the edging will blend in with the panel. Rip the edging ⅛ inch wider than the panel thickness.

3 Lastly, you'll glue the edging in place. First, cut lengths of edging that are about 1 inch longer than the edges they'll cover. Edge the top and bottom of each door first. Apply glue to the edge, and then put the edging in place so that it overhangs the panel on all sides. Secure the edging to the panel using masking tape. After the glue has set, saw each end of the edging flush with the sides of the door. Use a block plane to pare the edging flush with the faces of the door. Now install the edging on the sides of the door the same way.

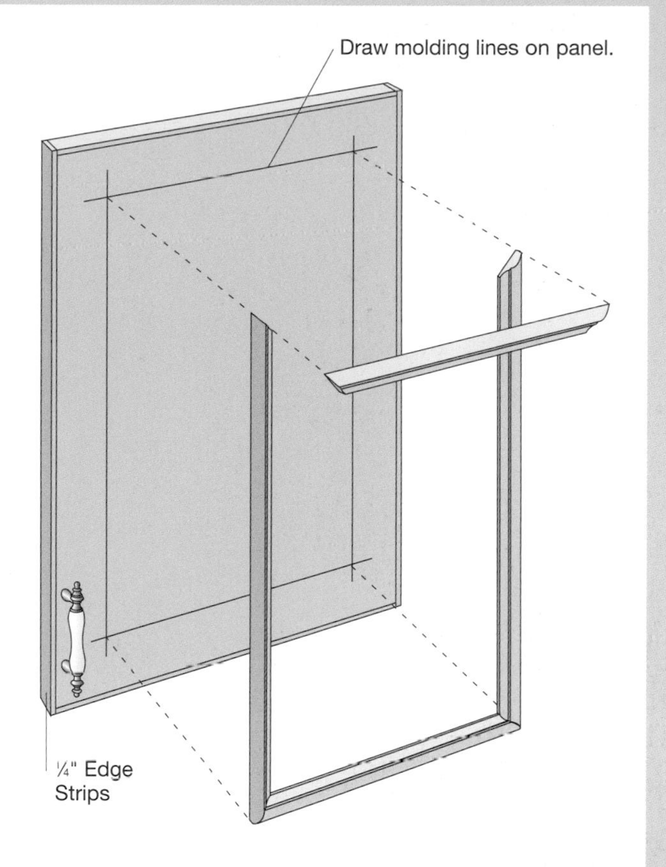
Draw molding lines on panel.
¼" Edge Strips

Installing Inset Doors

1 After you have installed the cabinet, measure the door opening and add ½ inch to the height and ½ inch to the width. This will give you a ⅜-inch-wide lip while giving the inset portion of the door ⅛ inch of clearance all around.

2 Use a router and a ⅜-inch rabbeting bit to mill a ⅜-deep rabbet along all four sides of the back of the door. Then if you like, use a ⅜-inch roundover bit to round over the front edges of the door.

3 Mark the locations of screw holes, and drill pilot holes. Install the hinges.

4 Hold the door in position in the cabinet, and mark the locations of the hinges and screw holes. Drill pilot holes, and hang the door.

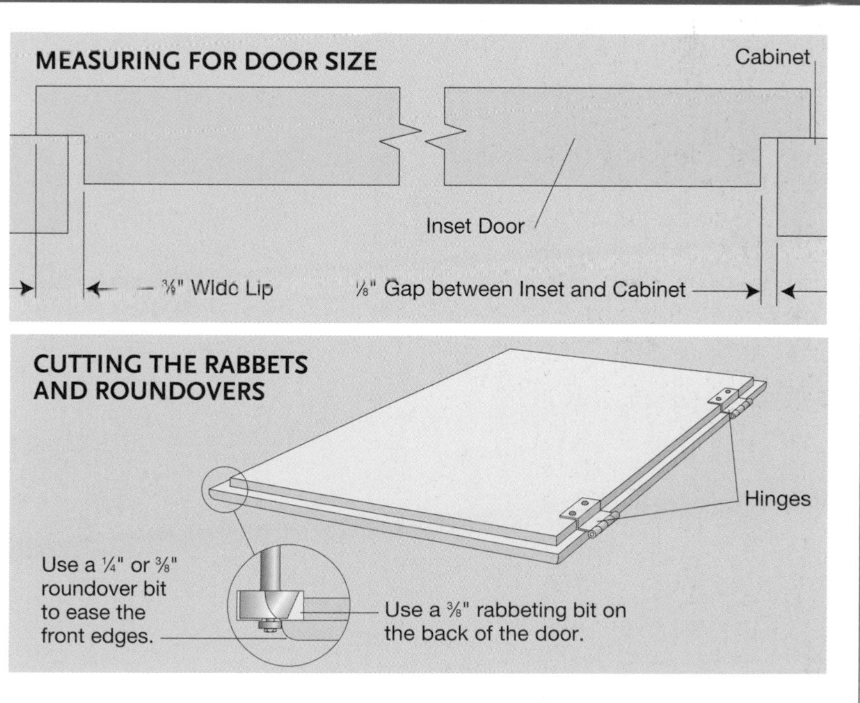
MEASURING FOR DOOR SIZE
Cabinet
Inset Door
⅜" Wide Lip
⅛" Gap between Inset and Cabinet
CUTTING THE RABBETS AND ROUNDOVERS
Hinges
Use a ¼" or ⅜" roundover bit to ease the front edges.
Use a ⅜" rabbeting bit on the back of the door.

Installing Flush-Fit Doors

For flush-fit doors, it's always a good idea to make them after you make the cabinets, so you can fit them to the actual size of the cabinet. If the cabinet will be built-in, install it before you install the door. After installing the cabinet, make sure that the frame is plumb and level before hanging the doors. Doors hung before cabinet installation could bind if the cabinet flexes.

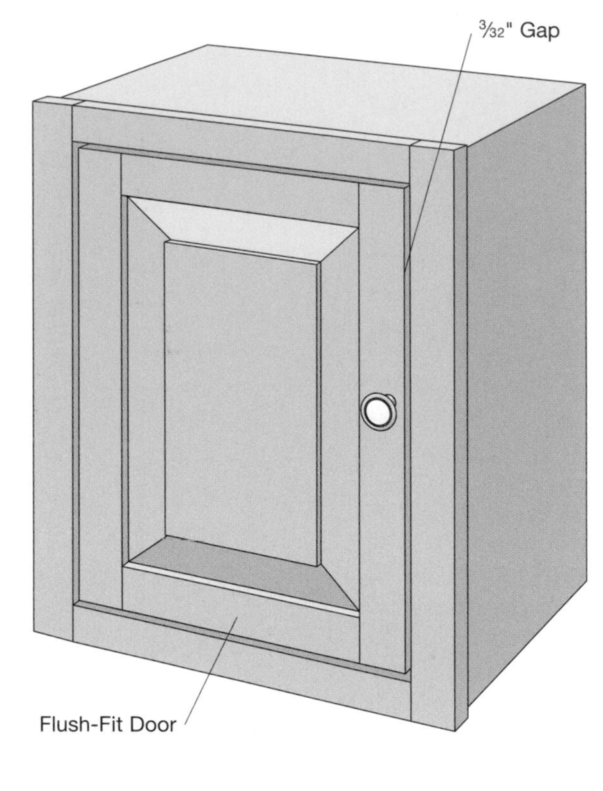

1 Fit the door by measure the height and width of each door. Allow yourself a 3⁄32-in. gap on all edges. To make installation a little easier, some cabinetmakers bevel the edges of flush-fit doors 3 to 5 deg. toward the back.

Doors & Hinges

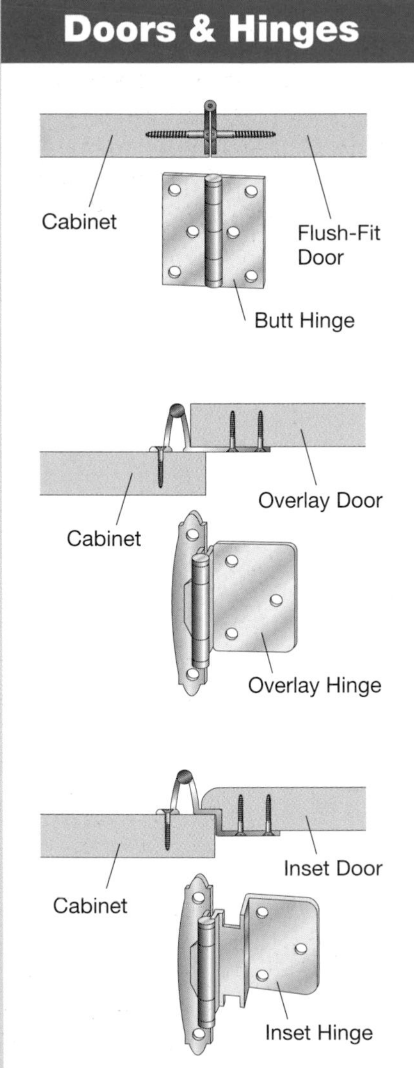

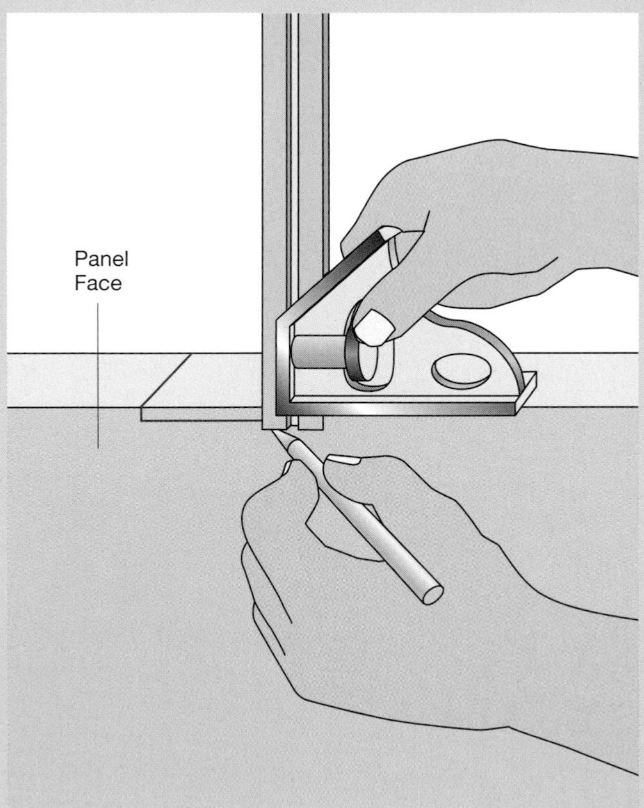

3 If the hinges you choose must be mortised into the door, start by clamping the door in a bench vise with the edge to be mortised facing up. Position the hinge on the door, and score the perimeter with a knife. Remove the hinge, and carefully deepen the score cuts to the depth of the hinge. Then use the thickness of one hinge leaf to set the ruler on a combination square. Use the square and a knife as shown to score the hinge depth on the face of the door.

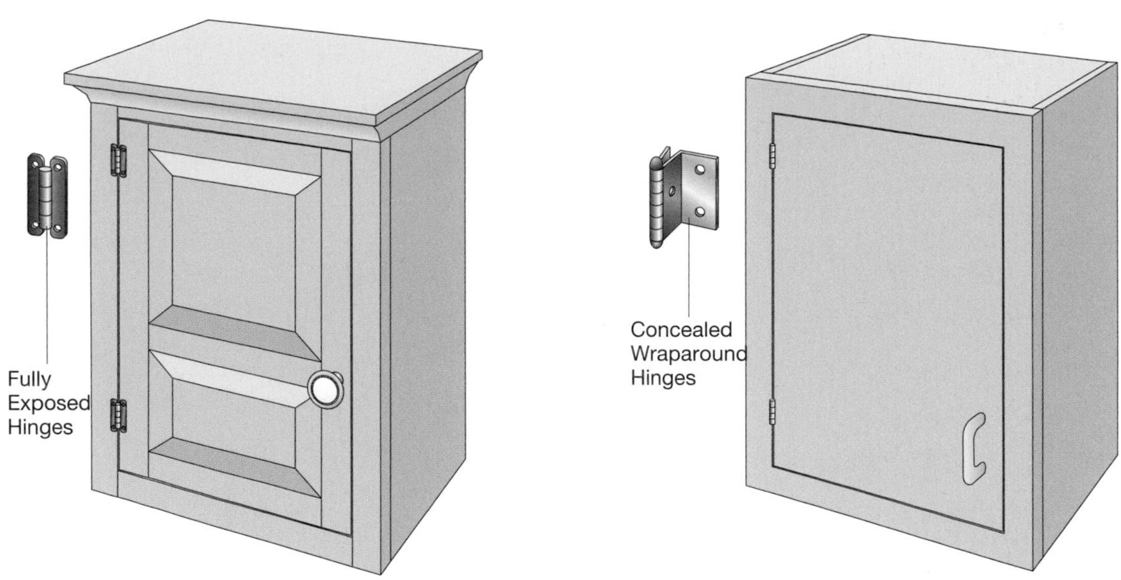
Fully
Exposed
Hinges
Concealed
Wraparound
Hinges

2 With solid-wood doors or doors with solid-wood frames, you can use butt hinges. Or for a more Colonial look, you can use fully exposed hinges as shown here. Butt hinges are unsuitable for plywood or particleboard doors because these materials aren't strong enough to support fasteners in their edges. You can use fully exposed hinges for plywood or particleboard, but flat panel doors such as these usually look better with a concealed wraparound hinge, as shown above right. Attach whichever hinges you choose to the door. The position of the hinges along the length of the door is mostly an aesthetic decision, but for best results you usually want to stay between 2 and 5 inches from the top and bottom of the door.

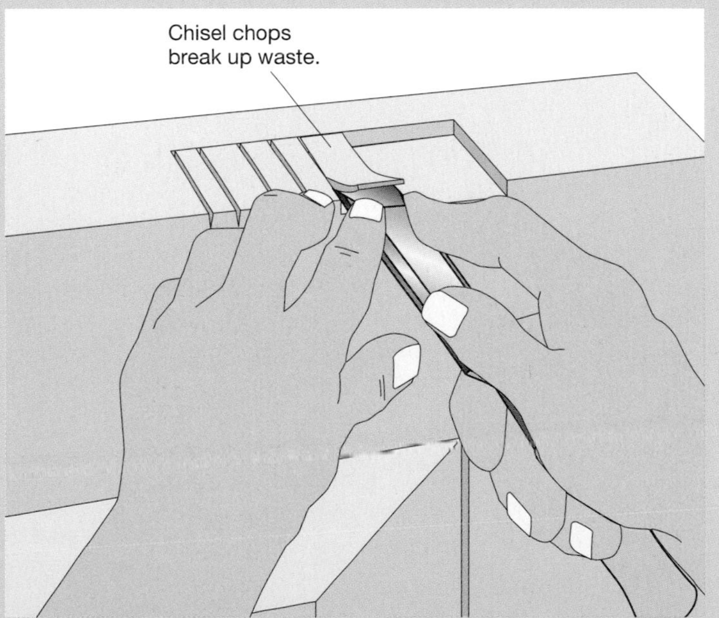
Chisel chops
break up waste.

4 Cut the mortises using a chisel. First, use a hammer and chisel to chop the waste areas into sections as shown in the illustration. Then use the chisel to pare out the waste. Make sure that the bevel side of the chisel faces up. When you have completed the mortise, mark the locations of screw holes and drill pilot holes. Install the hinges on the door.

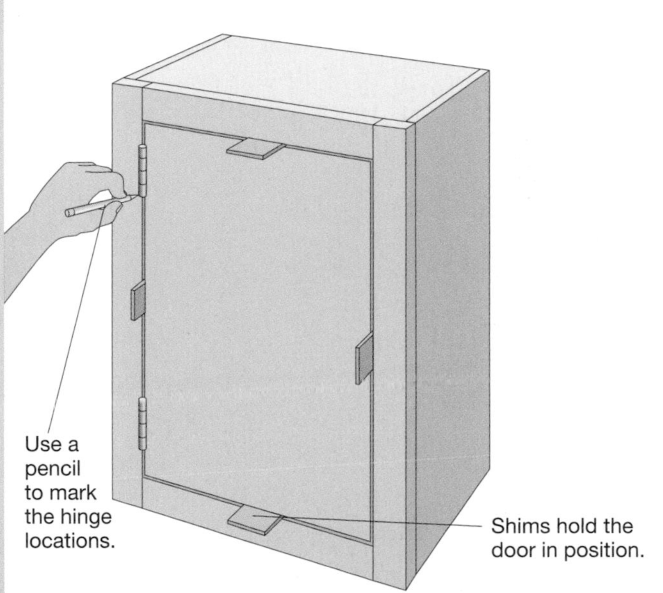
Use a
pencil
to mark
the hinge
locations.
Shims hold the
door in position.

5 Hold the door with hinges attached in position using shims. Then mark the hinge locations on the cabinet stile using a pencil. If you need to mortise the hinges into the cabinet, cut the outlines of the mortises using a knife. Cut the mortises with a chisel. Mark the screw holes, and drill pilot holes. Install the hinges and door.

Adjustable Cabinet Shelves

If you want to make cabinet shelves that are adjustable for height, there are two common ways to do it. One way is to use pins in holes drilled inside the cabinet; the other is to use metal shelf standards. Both are easy to use and install. Whichever you choose, check the hardware before you build your shelves. Different shelf-support hardware may require different clearances that may affect the size of the shelf.

Metal Standards

Cut shelf standards to length using a hacksaw. Cut them all off at the top end so that they will align with each other when registered to the bottom of the cabinet. Shelf standards can simply be screwed to the inside of the cabinet, but it is much more elegant to inset them into grooves. Cut the grooves on a table saw as described in "Making Dadoes and Grooves with a Table Saw," page 94.

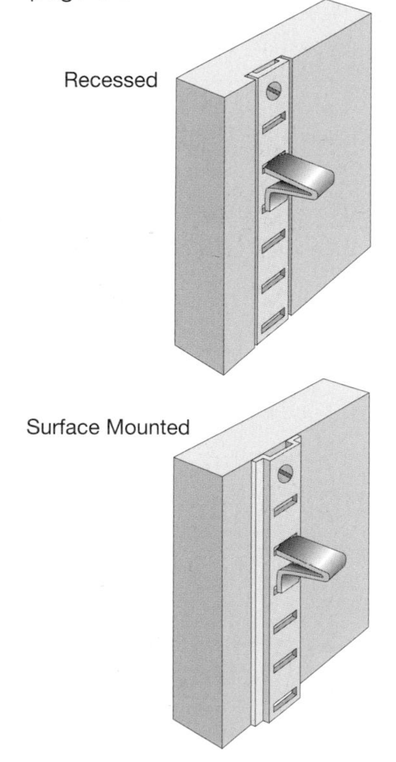

Installing Shelf Pins

Shelf pins come in a variety of styles. Some include brass insets that you tap into the holes, dressing them up a bit and making them more durable. Most shelf pins require a ¼-inch-diameter hole, but this varies.

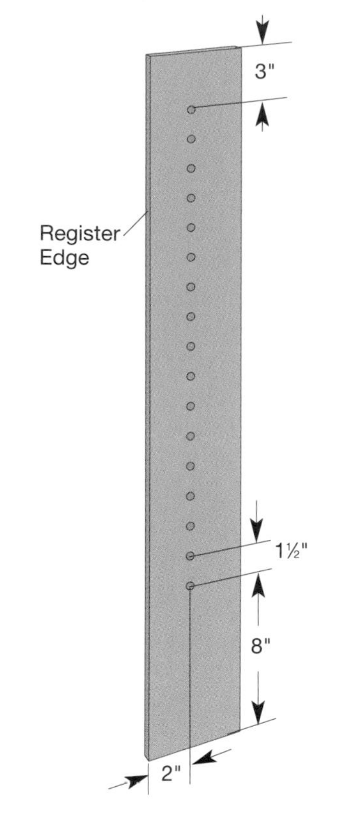

1 The trick to drilling holes for shelf pins is making sure every set of four holes is in perfect horizontal alignment. If they aren't aligned horizontally, the shelves will rock. If the holes are slightly misaligned to the front and back of the cabinet, it won't affect their function.

To ensure perfect horizontal alignment, make a simple drilling template from a scrap of ¼-inch-thick plywood. Rip the scrap to about 5 or 6 inches wide, and make it about 5 inches shorter than the inside height of the cabinet. Mark one long edge of the template as the "register edge." On this template, lay out the hole spacing you want. A good spacing is to make the holes two inches from the register edge. Lay out the first hole about 8 inches from the bottom of the template; then lay out a hole about every 1½ inches from the bottom of the template. Stop about 3 inches from the top of the template.

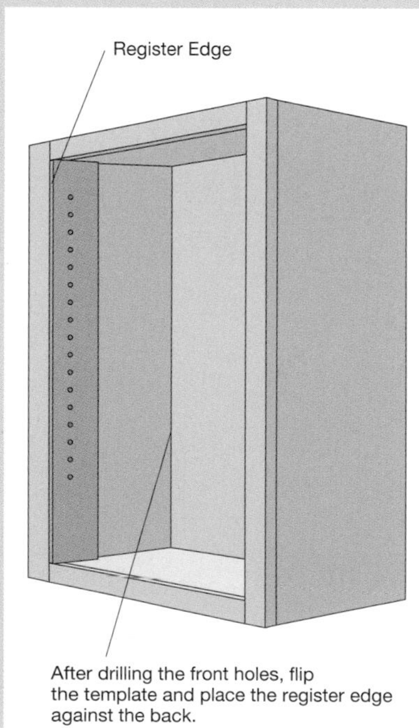

After drilling the front holes, flip the template and place the register edge against the back.

2 You should drill the holes using a stop collar or a piece of tape on the drill bit to mark the depth you want to drill. Align the register edge of the drilling template with the front edge of the cabinet. Make sure that the bottom of the template rests on the bottom of the cabinet. Clamp the template in place, and drill the holes. Now flip the drilling template over so that you'll be drilling through the other side. Push the register edge against the back of the cabinet. Drill the holes. Repeat this process for the holes in the opposing panel.

Catches and Latches

Catches and latches, usually made of brass or wrought iron, provide a rustic look. Mechanical or magnetic catches provide a cleaner, modern look. These catches consist of one part that attaches to the inside of the door and another that mounts inside the cabinet. Another choice is called a push latch, or touch latch. It is a spring-loaded magnetic device that holds the door closed and pops it open when the door is pushed.

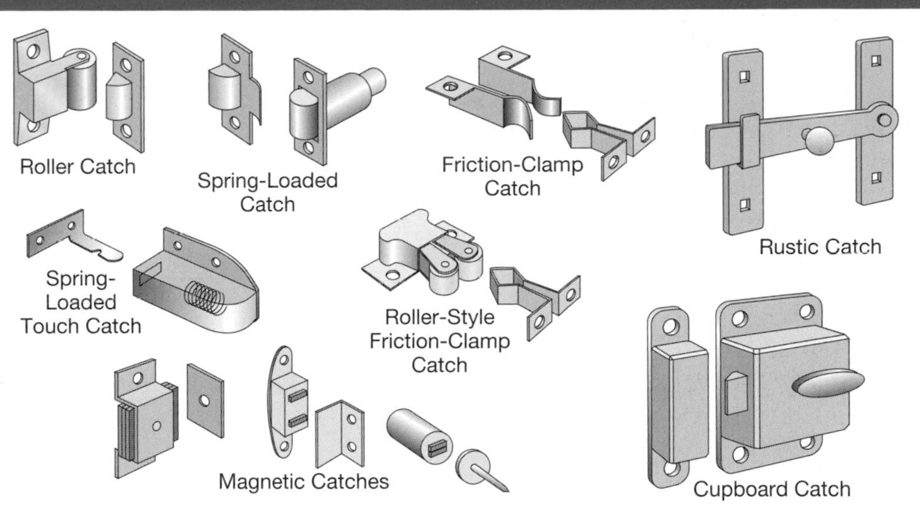

Drawer Slides

For furniture projects, you'll want to make your own wooden drawer slides. For kitchen and bathroom cabinet drawers, however, you may opt for commercial slides. These metal slides come in dozens of designs for bottom and side mounting. The smoothest operate on ball-bearing wheels or roller-bearing sleeves. For heavy-duty applications, you'll find slides rated for capacities of 75 to 100 pounds.

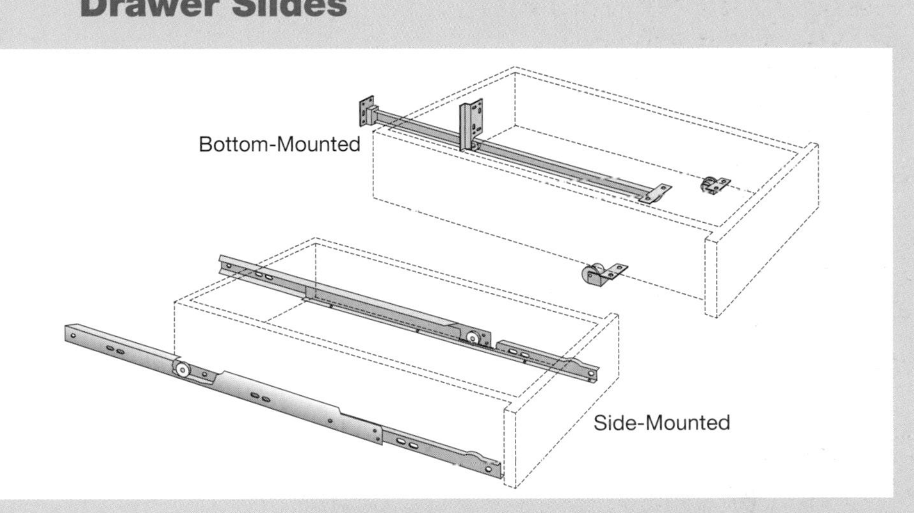

Hinges

Hardware for hanging cabinet doors is available in basic types for overlay, inset, and flush-fit, as well as designs for special purposes, such as concealed mounting and mounting on glass. There are plain hinges, and decorative hinges, and hinges that automatically close the door. Several types of cabinets use piano, or continuous, hinges, which are available in lengths up to 72 inches and can be cut with a hacksaw to any length you need.

Butt Hinge

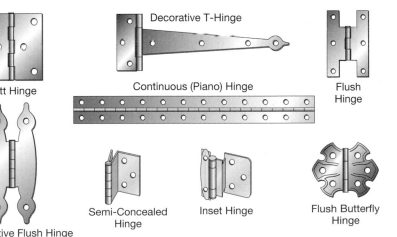

Decorative T-Hinge

Flush Hinge

Continuous (Piano) Hinge

Decorative Flush Hinge

Semi-Concealed Hinge

Inset Hinge

Flush Butterfly Hinge

Rollout Shelf

Some base cabinets can be a pain in the back, especially when you try to reach pots, pans, or other items stored in them—invariably, whatever you're reaching for is at the very back of the cabinet. If you're tired of being a kitchen contortionist and unloading cabinets just to reach a sauce pan or to lift out a heavy food processor, this rollout shelf is the prescription for your relief. You'll probably want to make and install several of them.

The shelf featured here is sized to fit into a cabinet that is 18 inches wide and 24 inches deep. To support the shelf, install it in a cabinet that is made of ¾-inch-thick plywood with 1 ½-inch-wide face frames because the rollout shelf uses ¾-inch-thick wood slide hangers to allow the shelf to slide past the face frames. If you are installing the rollout shelf in cabinets that have a ¾-inch-wide face frame or no face frame at all, omit the slide hangers.

The rollout shelf uses side-mounted metal drawer slides. Typically, these slides require ½ inch of clearance on each side. This leaves you with an overall shelf width of 20 inches. To accommodate wider or narrower openings and deeper or shallower cabinets, adjust shelf dimensions to suit your needs.

Roll-Out Shelf Material List

Difficulty Level: EASY

Quantity	Part	Dimensions	Quantity	Part
2	Solid-wood sides	¾" x 3" x 22½"	***Hardware***	
1	Solid-wood back	¾" x 3" x 14"		¾" Brads
1	Plywood bottom	½" x 13¼" x 22½"		#6 x 1¼" Wood screws
2	Guide hangers	¾" x 4" x 22⅞"	1 set	22" Side-mounted metal drawer slides

Overall View of Rollout Shelf

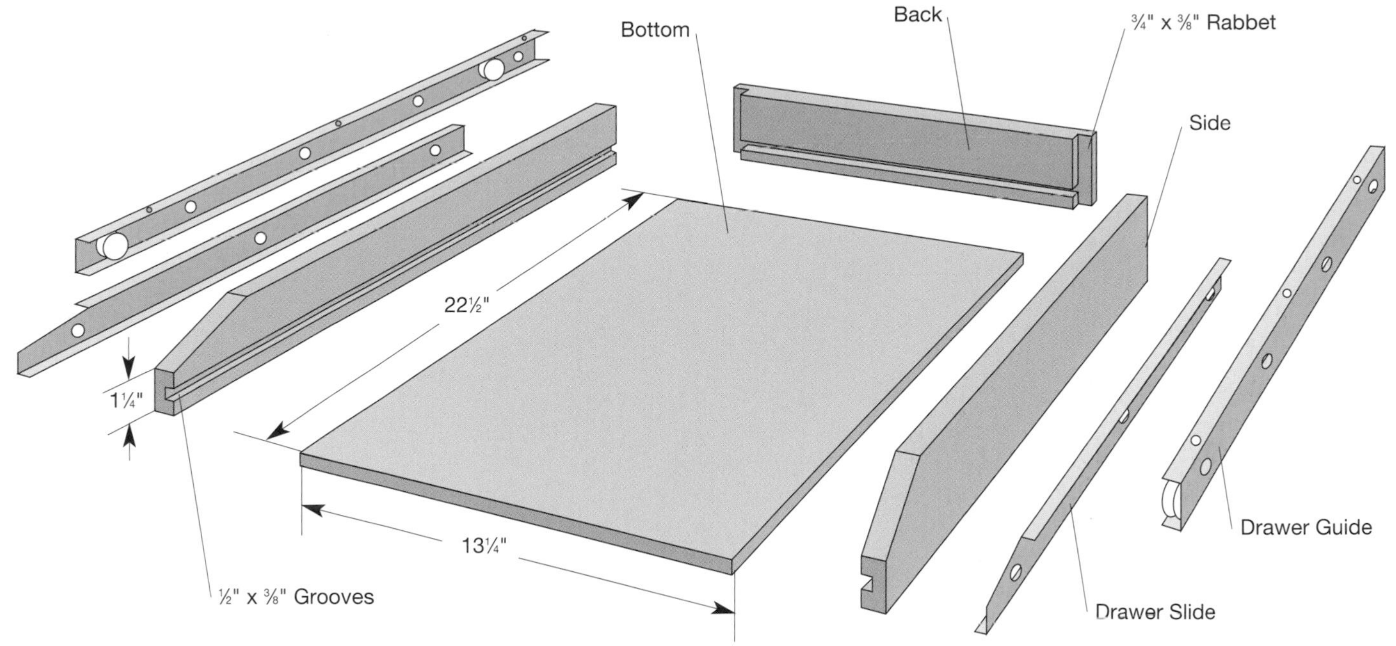

Bottom
Back
¾" x ⅜" Rabbet
Side
22½"
1¼"
13¼"
½" x ⅜" Grooves
Drawer Guide
Drawer Slide

Building the Shelf

1 Cut the parts. Cut sides, back, bottom, and slide hangers to the dimensions in the Materials List. Then cut off the top front corner of each side. Make the cut at a 45-degree angle, 1¼ inches up from the bottom front corner.

2 Groove and rabbet the sides and back. Cut grooves in the sides and back as shown in the Overall View. Then cut rabbets into the ends of the back panel. (See "Making Dadoes and Grooves with a Table Saw," page 94; and "Making Rabbets with a Table Saw," page 95.)

3 Assemble the shelf. Sand all parts before assembly. Assemble the shelf using glue and ¾-inch brads. Clamp it using bar or pipe clamps, and let it stand until the glue sets.

4 Apply the finish. Sand the shelf, and apply the finish of your choice. Allow the finish to dry.

Installing the Slides and Shelf

1 Install the guide hangers. If the rollout shelf will be installed directly over an existing fixed shelf, simply attach the slide hangers directly on top of the shelf using glue and countersink 1¼-inch wood screws into the cabinet sides as shown in Shelf Installation. Otherwise, draw level lines where you want the shelf to go, and attach the hangers along those lines.

2 Attach the slides and glides. Following the manufacturer's directions, attach drawer slides to the rollout shelf using the screws provided. Fasten the drawer guides to the cabinet side panels using the screws provided. Make sure the guides are level both front to back and with each other.

Shelf Installation

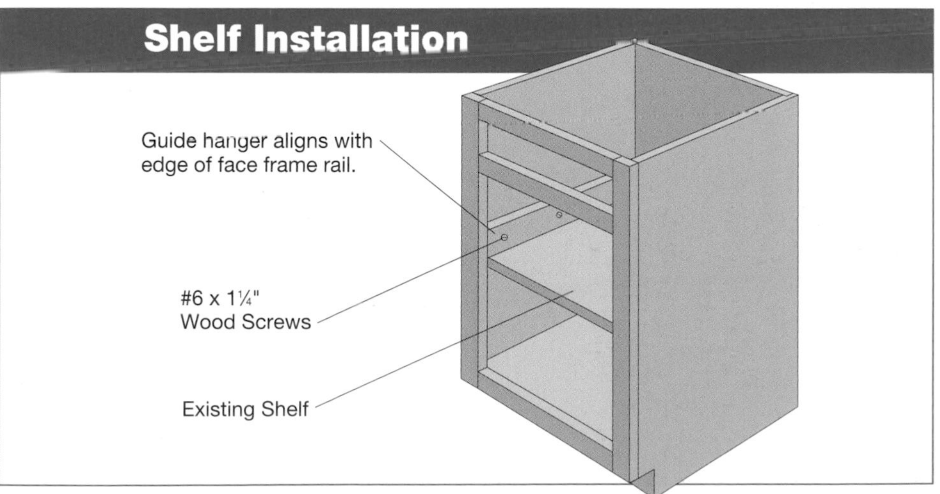
Guide hanger aligns with edge of face frame rail.
#6 x 1¼" Wood Screws
Existing Shelf

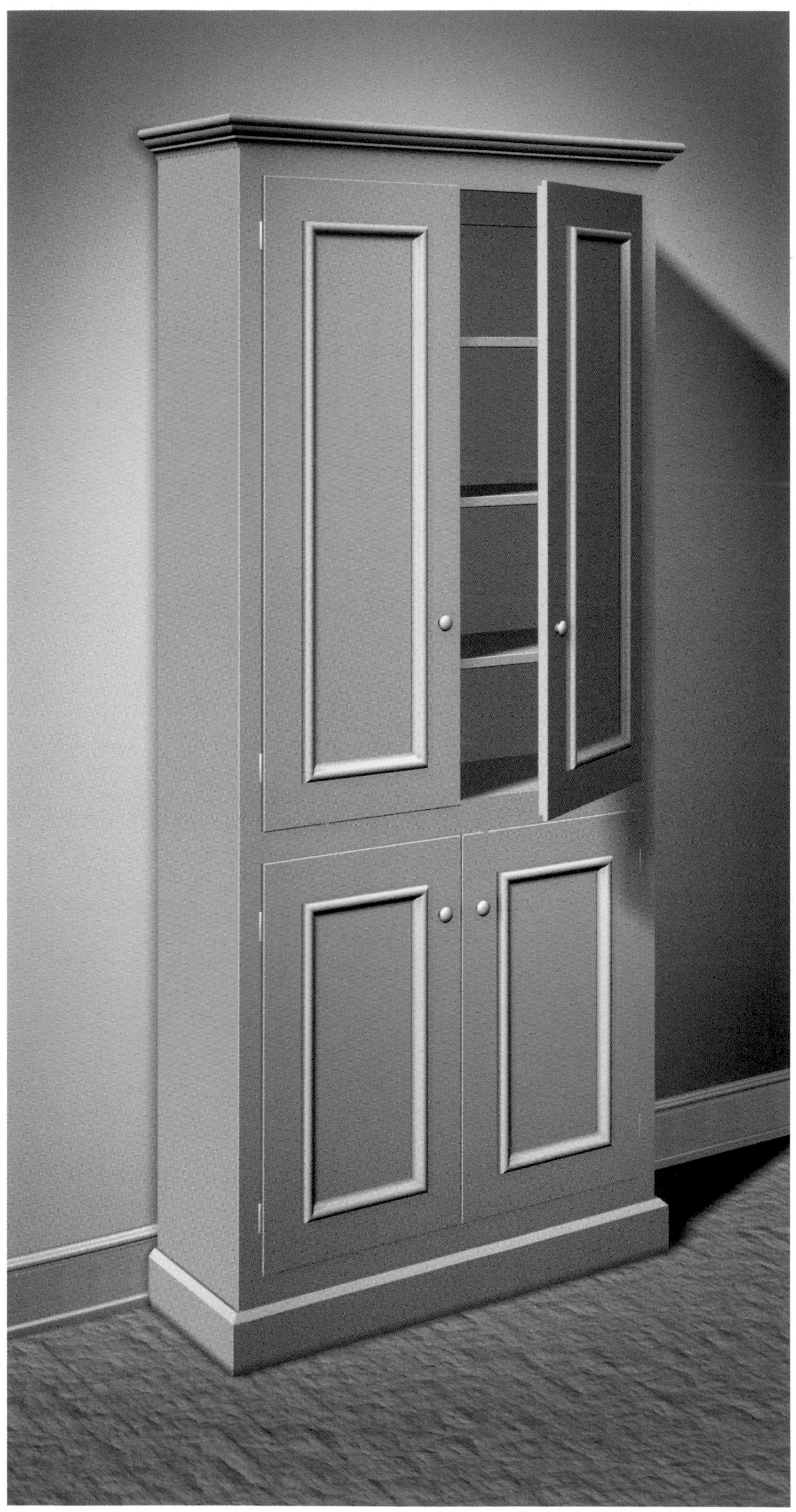

Linen Cabinet

Finding space to store towels and bed linen is a common problem. Although most home layouts do include a linen closet, these are often quite small and can quickly become inadequate as families grow and new purchases are made. And most linen closets end up serving as storage for other items as well—toiletries, cleaning supplies, and the like. To compound the problem, it is hard to find space in the typical home to add a full closet to act as a buffer. This linen cabinet was designed with these problems in mind. It is shallow enough that you could place it in areas you might otherwise consider unsuitable for storage. It can fit within a bathroom or bedroom without sacrificing valuable floor space, or you might even use it in a wide hallway or on a landing, providing there is enough room to meet building code safety requirements.

The construction details of the cabinet are intentionally very simple. It is designed to be built using paint-grade materials, such as birch plywood and poplar or pine lumber, although you could certainly substitute a more attractive hardwood species and apply a clear or stained finish if that better fits your decor. And you can personalize your cabinet somewhat by your choice of the applied panel molding that adorns the cabinet doors. While our model cabinet shows a simple molding profile, you will find a wide selection of possible moldings at any home center or lumberyard, and you can easily substitute one that appeals to you—it wouldn't even be necessary to adjust the dimensions shown in the Materials List.

Linen Cabinet Material List

Difficulty Level: CHALLENGING

Quantity	Part	Dimensions
Carcase		
2	Plywood sides	¾" x 11¼" x 83¼"
2	Plywood fixed shelves	¾" x 11" x 35"
1	Top	¾" x 13⅝" x 39¼"
	1 Plywood top panel	¾" x 13½" x 38¼"
	1 Solid-wood edging	½" x ¾" x 39¼"
	2 Solid-wood edging	½" x ¾" x 13⅝"
1	Plywood back	¼" x 35½" x 78 5/16"
2	Solid-wood nailers	¾" x 5¼" x 35½"
1	Bed molding	9/16" x 1¾" x 38¼"
2	Bed molding	9/16" x 1¾" x 13⅛"
1	Solid-wood baseboard	¾" x 4" x 37½"
2	Solid-wood baseboard	¾" x 4" x 12¾"
5	Adjustable shelves	¾" x 10⅞" x 34⅜"
	5 Plywood shelf panels	¾" x 10⅛" x 34⅜"
	5 Solid-wood edging	½" x ¾" x 34⅜"
1	Shoe molding (opt.)	½" x ¾" x 38½"
2	Shoe molding (opt.)	½" x ¾" x 13¼"
Face Frame		
2	Solid-wood stiles	¾" x 2" x 83¾"
1	Solid-wood top rail	¾" x 3½" x 32"
1	Solid-wood middle rail	¾" x 2⅝" x 32"
1	Solid-wood bottom rail	¾" x 5¼" x 32"

Quantity	Part	Dimensions
Doors		
2	Upper doors	¾" x 16 3/16" x 44¼"
	2 Plywood door panels	¾" x 15 3/16" x 43¼"
	4 Solid-wood edging	½" x ¾" x 16 3/16"
	4 Solid-wood edging	½" x ¾" x 44¼"
	4 Panel molding	⅝" x 1¼" x 10 3/16"
	4 Panel molding	⅝" x 1¼" x 38¼"
2	Lower doors	¾" x 16 3/16" x 27⅝"
	2 Plywood door panels	¾" x 15 3/16" x 26⅝"
	4 Solid-wood edging	½" x ¾" x 16 3/16"
	4 Solid-wood edging	½" x ¾" x 27⅝"
	4 Panel molding	⅝" x 1¼" x 10 3/16"
	4 Panel molding	⅝" x 1¼" x 21⅝"
Hardware and Miscellaneous Supplies		
4 pr.	⅜" rabbet/overlay self-closing door hinges	
4	door knobs	
4	29¾" metal-shelf standards	
4	47 5/16" metal-shelf standards	
20	metal-shelf clips	
14	¼" x 1½" wood dowels	
	1" brads	
	4 and 6d finishing nails	

Building the Carcase

1 Cut the parts. Cut plywood and solid stock to the dimensions shown in the Materials List for the sides, top, back, fixed shelves, and nailers.

2 Cut the dadoes and rabbets. Use router with straight bit to cut the ¼-inch-deep dadoes in the case sides for the fixed shelves. (See "Making Dadoes with the Router," page 96.) Next, you can use the router with a straightedge guide to cut the rabbet along the back edge of each side panel to house the case back. Mark the limits of the stopped rabbet on the top panel; then use the router to cut that as well. Stop the router bit about ⅛-inch shy of the end marks, and use a sharp chisel to square the ends of the cut.

Mark the outlines of the wide rabbets for the top and bottom nailers in the side panels; then use the router to cut these recesses. Once again, stop the cut about ⅛-inch shy of the inside corner marks, and use a sharp chisel to finish the cuts.

Install a ⅝-inch-wide straight-cutting router bit into the router, and cut the grooves for shelf standards in the cabinet side panels.

3 Apply edging to the top. Cut the 45-degree miter joints on edging strips for the case top. Spread glue on the top panel edges, and apply the strips, using masking tape as a clamp to hold the strips in position while the glue sets.

4 Assemble the carcase. Spread glue in the shelf dadoes in the case sides; then join the sides to the shelves. Use 6d finishing nails to fasten these joints. Apply glue to the nailer rabbets, and slide the nailers into position. Drive finishing nails through the case sides to fix them in place. Next, spread glue on the top ends of the side panels, and place he top in position. Check that it overhangs equally on both ends; then fasten it using 6d finishing nails.

Lay the carcase on its face, and check that the assembly is square by comparing opposite diagonal measurements. (See "Squaring a Carcase," page 98.) Spread glue on the rabbets in the top and side panels and on the back edges of the shelves; then slide the back panel into position; and fasten it by nailing using 1-inch brads.

5 Build and install the face frame. Cut the stiles and rails to the dimensions shown in the Materials List. Mark the positions of dowels for the face frame joints; then use a doweling jig to bore the required holes. (See "Reinforcing Joints with Dowels," page 93.) Apply glue to the holes and also on each dowel; then assemble the face frame. Use bar clamps to pull the joints tight; then check that the frame is square by comparing opposite diagonal measurements; adjust the clamps if necessary to bring the assembly square.

Continued on next page.

Continued from previous page.

6 Lay the carcase on its back, and spread glue on the front edges of the shelves and sides. Put the face frame into position, and nail it to the case parts using 6d finishing nails. You can also nail through the case top into the edge of the top rail.

7 Install the moldings. Cut the bed and base moldings to size with 45-degree angles for the front miter joints. Use 4d finishing nails to fasten the moldings in place—remember to apply glue to the mating surfaces of the miters to ensure that the joints stay tight.

8 Install the shelf tracks. Cut metal shelf tracks to length as shown in the Materials List. Install them in the dadoes in case sides using the screws or nails provided with the hardware.

Building the Doors

1 Cut the parts. Cut door panels, edging strips, and panel moldings to the sizes shown in the Materials list. Use a miter saw to trim the ends of the edging strips and molding, which must be cut at 45-degree angles to form miter joints at the corners.

2 Apply the edging strips. Spread glue on the door panel edges; place the edging strips into position; and clamp them to the door using strips of masking tape. Allow the glue to cure for at least 30 minutes before removing the tape.

3 Rabbet the door edges. Use a router with a rabbeting bit or a table saw with dado blades to cut the rabbets on three sides of each door panel as shown in the plans. (See also "Installing Inset Doors," page 99.) Remember that the edges of the doors that meet in the center of the cabinet do not need to be rabbeted—only those edges that overlay the face frame.

Overall View of Carcase

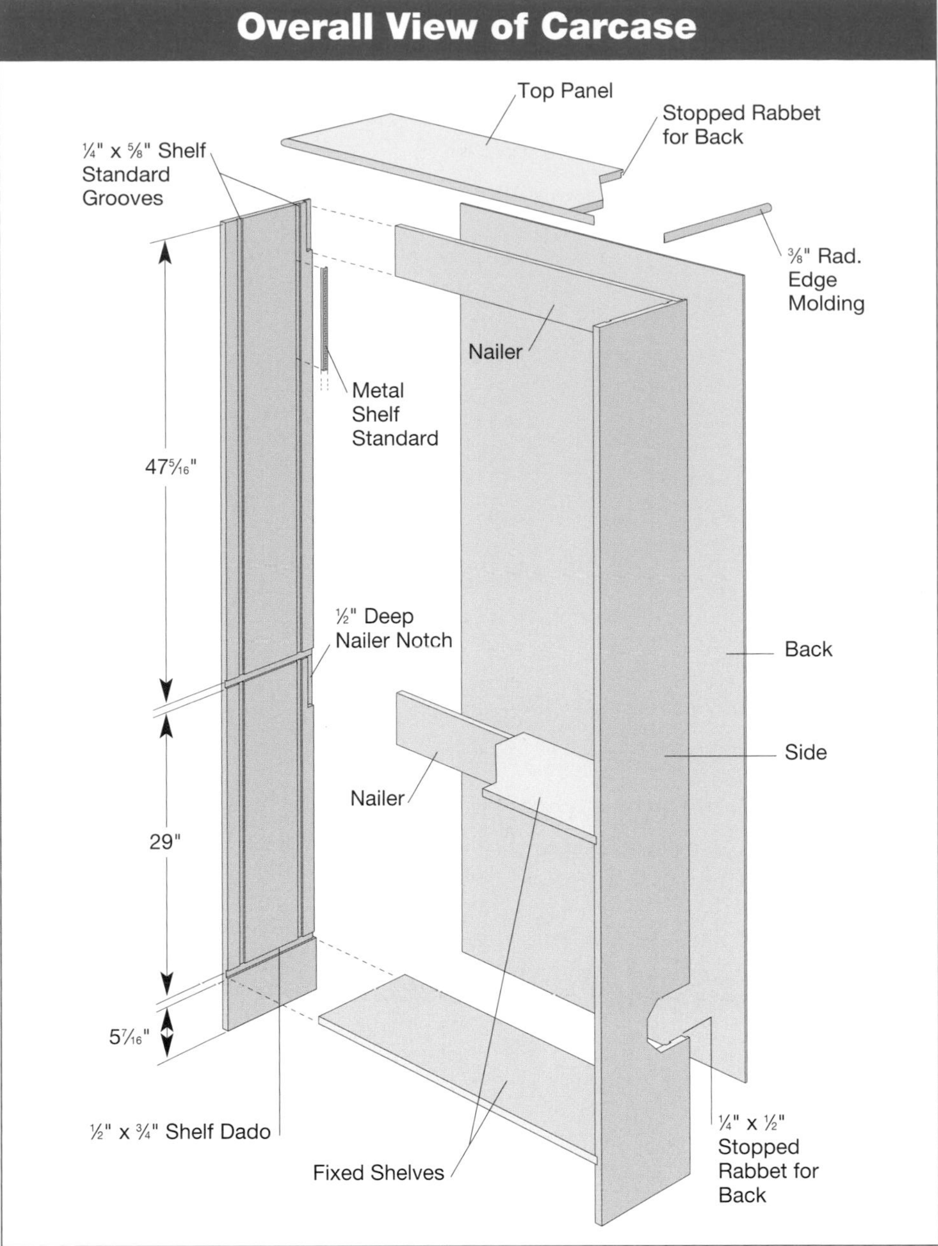

4 Apply the panel molding. Mark the surface of the door to indicate the outer edges of the panel molding strips. Apply a small amount of glue to the back side of the molding; then use 1-inch brads to fasten it to the door panel. (See "Building a Slab Door," page 99.)

5 Install the doors. Mark the locations of screw holes for the hinges on each door; then drill pilot holes. Mount the hinges to the door panels using the screws provided. Hold the doors in position on the cabinet to mark the screw locations. Drill pilot holes, and mount the doors. Determine the location of door knobs; drill pilot holes; and mount the hardware.

Making the Adjustable Shelves

1 Cut the parts. Cut the plywood shelves and edging strips to the sizes listed in the Materials List.

2 Apply edging strips. Spread glue on the front edge of each shelf panel, and clamp the edging strips in place using masking tape.

Face Frame, Door, and Trim Details

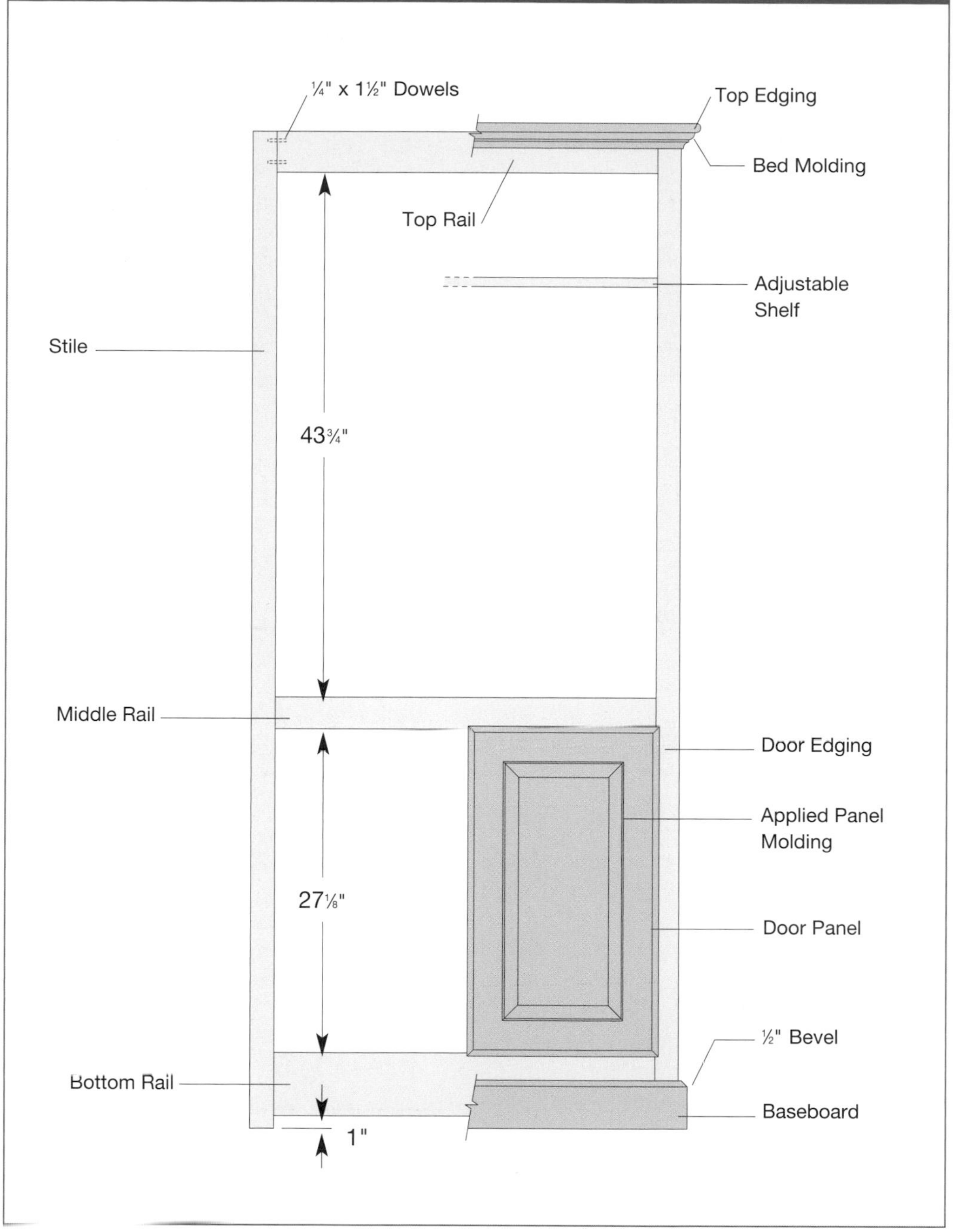

¼" x 1½" Dowels
Top Edging
Bed Molding
Top Rail
Adjustable Shelf
Stile
43¾"
Middle Rail
Door Edging
Applied Panel Molding
27⅛"
Door Panel
½" Bevel
Bottom Rail
Baseboard
1"

Door Top Section View

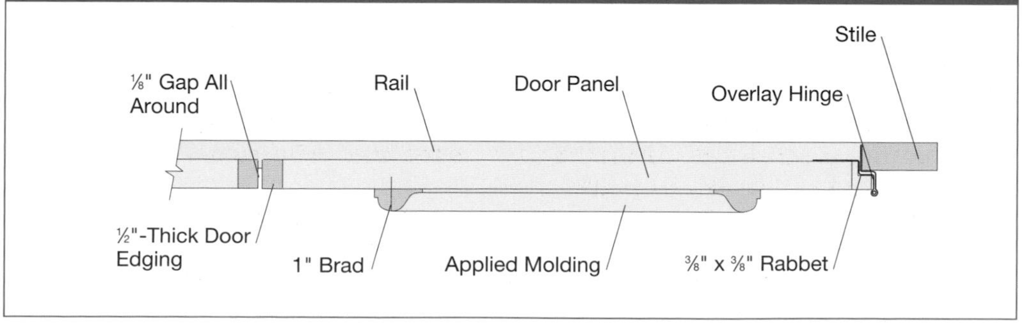

Stile
⅛" Gap All Around
Rail
Door Panel
Overlay Hinge
½"-Thick Door Edging
1" Brad
Applied Molding
⅜" x ⅜" Rabbet

Finishing the Cabinet

1 Remove the shelves and doors. To make finishing easier, temporarily remove the doors and adjustable shelves from the cabinet.

2 Prep all parts. Set all nailheads below the wood surface, and fill the holes with drying wood filler. Mound the filler slightly over the surface to allow for shrinkage while it dries. Sand all cabinet parts using 120-, 150-, and 220-grit sandpaper, remembering to remove the sanding dust whenever you switch to a finer grit paper.

3 Apply the finish of your choice. Follow the manufacturer's directions for the product you choose.

4 Install the cabinet. Place the cabinet against the wall in the desired location. If there is baseboard molding on the wall, you will first need to remove it to allow the cabinet to fit flush to the wall surface. Use a spirit level to check that the cabinet is level and plumb. You can use small, tapered shingles to adjust the position of the cabinet if necessary. Drive screws through the top and bottom nailer strips inside the cabinet to fasten the case to the wall studs. Reinstall the baseboard molding to the wall on either side of the cabinet. If you placed shims under the cabinet to bring it level, you can now install shoe molding around the case to hide any gaps between the baseboard and finished floor surface.

Install the adjustable shelves, and remount the cabinet doors to complete the installation.

glossary

Backsplash The finish material that covers the wall behind a countertop. The backsplash can be attached to the countertop or separate from it.
Base cabinet A cabinet that rests on the floor and supports a countertop.
Butt joint A joint with one piece of wood simply butted against the other.
Carcase The basic case of a cabinet.
Carpenter's wood glue Aliphatic resin glue used for bonding wood to wood.
Carousel shelves Revolving shelves that are usually installed in corner cabinets.
Combination square A graduated steel blade with a sliding handle that can be tightened at any position.
Contact cement A rubber-based liquid glue that bonds on contact.
Corner clamps Clamps designed to hold two pieces of material together at a right angle.
Countertop The work surface of a counter, island, or peninsula, usually 36 inches high. Common countertop materials include plastic laminate, ceramic tile, slate, and solid surfacing.
Crosscut A cut that is made across the grain on a piece of wood.
Dado A type of groove that runs across the grain.
Dado blade A special blade used on a table saw to make dadoes.
Depth stop On a drill, a collar that stops the bit when it reaches a desired depth.
Edge-gluing A technique in which two or several boards are bonded together edge-to-edge to form a panel.
Face frame A frame of stiles and rails that is applied to the face of a cabinet for style and strength.
Featherboard A single piece of wood with slots cut into one end. Featherboards are safety devices clamped to the work surface of certain power tools.
Framed cabinets Cabinets with a full frame across the face of the cabinet box.
Frameless cabinets European-style cabinets without a face frame.
Grain The direction and arrangement of wood fibers in a piece of wood.
Groove A channel cut into a piece of wood that runs with the grain.
Grout A mixture of Portland cement and water—and sometimes sand—used to fill the gaps between ceramic tiles.
Hardwood Wood that comes from deciduous trees (those that lose their leaves in fall).
Island A base cabinet and countertop unit that stands independent from walls, so that there is access from all four sides.
Jig A device for holding a workpiece, or attached to a workpiece, that allows a tool to cut the workpiece safely and accurately.
Kickback The dangerous action that happens when a saw suddenly jumps backward out of a cut or when a stationary power saw throws a piece of wood back at the operator.
Knockdown cabinets Cabinets that are shipped flat and assembled on the building site.
Lazy susan Axis-mounted shelves that revolve. Also called carousel shelves.
Lumber grade A label that reflects the lumber's natural growth characteristics (such as knots) and defects that result from milling errors.
Miter joint A joint in which the ends of two boards are cut at equal angles (typically 45 degrees) to form a corner.
Nail set A pointed tool with one round or square end, used to drive nails flush with or below the surface of wood.
Nominal dimensions The identifying dimensions of a piece of lumber (e.g., 2x4) which are larger than the actual dimensions (1½ x 3½).
Peninsula A countertop, with or without a base cabinet, that is connected at one end to a wall or another countertop and extends outward, providing access on three sides.

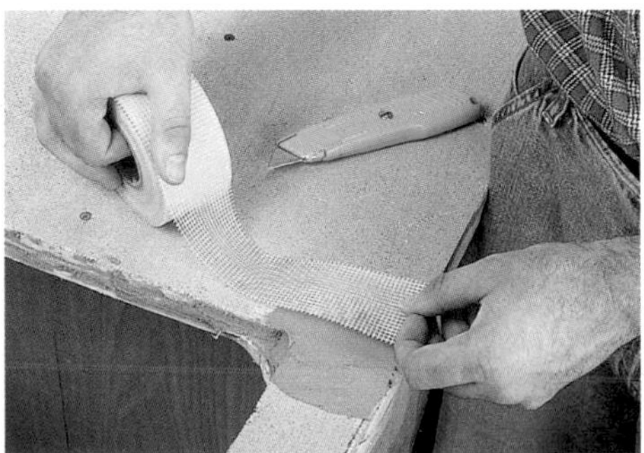

Plastic laminate A hard-surface, thin material made from melamine under high pressure and used for the finished surfaces of countertops, cabinets, flooring, and furniture.
Plywood Veneers of wood glued together in a sandwich. Each veneer is oriented perpendicularly to the next.
Rabbet A ledge cut along one edge of a workpiece.
Rail A horizontal member that is placed between stiles.
Raised panel A board with bevels on all four sides on one face so that stock is thicker in the center than at its perimeter.
Refacing Replacing the doors and drawers on cabinets and covering the face frames with a matching material.
Rip cut A cut made with the grain on a piece of wood.
Rip fence An attachment to a table saw used to guide wood through a cut.
Router A power tool used to do such things as making grooves, dadoes, and rabbets, and mortising door hinges.
Shim A tapered piece of wood used to level and secure a structure.
Softwood Wood that comes from coniferous trees, such as evergreens.
Stile Vertical member placed perpendicular to rails.
Stud Vertical member of a frame wall, placed at both ends and usually every 16 inches on center.
T-bevel Also known as the sliding T-bevel or bevel square. A simple tool that consists of a handle or stock attached to a 6- or 8-inch slotted blade.
Table saw A stationary power saw that can be used for crosscutting, ripping (cutting a board along the grain from end to end), grooving, and joinery.
Traffic pattern The pattern of movement people use in a kitchen.
Try square A square with a broad blade attached to a stock at a right angle.
Under-cabinet light fixtures Light fixtures that are installed on the undersides of cabinets for task lighting.
Wood screws Screws that are tapered so that the threads bite into the wood.

index

Photo Credits

Illustrations by: Vincent Babak, Clarke Barre, Glee Barre, Frank Rohrbach, Paul M. Schumm, Ian Warpole

page 1: Mark Lohman, design: Roxanne Packham Design **page 3:** *top* courtesy of Kraftmaid; *center* Olson Photographic, LLC, design: Jack Rosen Custom Kitchens; *bottom* courtesy of CaesarStone **page 5:** *top* John Parsekian/CH; *bottom* Rob Melnychuk **page 6:** *top left* courtesy of Kraftmaid; *top right* courtesy of IKEA; *bottom right* courtesy of CaesarStone; *bottom left* courtesy of U-Line **page 7:** *(screwdrivers)* Hot99/Dreamstime.com; *all others* Neal Barrett/CH **page 8:** Gary David Gold/CH **page 9:** Brian C. Nieves/CH **page 10:** *top left* & *bottom right* H. Howard Hudgins, Jr./CH; *top right* & *bottom left* John Parsekian/CH **page 11:** H. Howard Hudgins, Jr./CH **page 12:** *top* H. Howard Hudgins, Jr./CH; *bottom both* Gary David Gold/CH **page 13:** *top* H. Howard Hudgins, Jr./CH; *center both* & *bottom* Gary David Gold/CH **page 14:** *top left* courtesy of Kitchens by Deane; *top right* Mark Samu; *bottom right* Olson Photographic, LLC, design: Cucina Designs; *bottom left* Mark Lohman **page 15–16:** *both* courtesy of Kraftmaid **page 17:** *left* Mark Samu, design: Jim DeLuca, AIA; *right* Eric Roth, design: Dahlia Kitchen Design **page 18:** *both* courtesy of Kraftmaid **page 19:** *all* courtesy of American Olean **page 20:** *top* courtesy of MasterBrand; *bottom* courtesy of IKEA **page 21:** *left* courtesy of Rev-A-Shelf; *right both* courtesy of Kraftmaid **page 22:** *left* courtesy of ALNO; *right both* courtesy of Merillat **page 23:** courtesy of Kraftmaid **page 24:** *all* courtesy of GarageTek **page 25:** *top* Tony Giammarino/Giammarino & Dworkin; *bottom* courtesy of Rubbermaid **page 26:** courtesy of Gladiator; *right inset* courtesy of GarageTek **page 27:** *top* Bradley Olman; *bottom* courtesy of The Container Store **page 28:** *top left* Freeze Frame Studio/CH; *top right* Olson Photographic, LLC, design/architect: design: Crosskey Architects, LLC; *bottom right* John Parsekian/CH; *bottom left* courtesy of Merillat **page 29:** *left* John Parsekian/CH; *right* Brian C. Nieves/CH **page 30–33:** *all* John Parsekian/CH **page 34–36:** *all* Freeze Frame Studio/CH **page 37:** *both* courtesy of Sears Cabinet Refacing **page 38–39:** *all* Freeze Frame Studio/CH **page 40–41:** *bottom left* courtesy of Osram Sylvania; *sequence all* Freeze Frame Studio/CH **page 42:** *top left* Mark Lohman, design: Roxanne Packham Design; *top right* Olson Photographic, LLC, design: Jack Rosen Custom Kitchens; *bottom right* courtesy of Formica; *bottom left* courtesy of EcoTop Surfaces by kliptech.com **page 43:** *left* courtesy of Kraftmaid; *right* davidduncanlivingston.com **page 44:** *top* Jerry Pavia, design: Ed Schramm Tile Work; *bottom right* davidduncanlivingston.com; *left* Tony Giammarino/Giammarino & Dworkin **page 45:** *top* courtesy of Moen; *bottom* davidduncanlivingston.com **page 46:** *top* courtesy of Kohler; *right center* courtesy of CaesarStone; *bottom right* Olson Photographic, LLC, design: Sally Scott Interiors; *left* davidduncanlivingston.com **page 47:** *both* Tony Giammarino/Giammarino & Dworkin, design: Kelly Stalls **page 48:** courtesy of IKEA **page 49:** *both* courtesy of Kohler **page 50:** *top* Mark Lohman; *bottom* courtesy of Moen **page 51:** courtesy of Kohler **page 52:** courtesy of Corian **page 53–55:** *all* Freeze Frame Studio/CH **page 56–57:** *all* John Parsekian/CH **page 58:** *left* John Parsekian/CH; *right* Mark Samu **page 59:** *all* John Parsekian/CH **page 60–61:** *left both* John Parsekian/CH; *right all* Freeze Frame Studio/CH **page 62–6 :** *all* Merle Henkenius/CH **page 64:** *top left* courtesy of Yorktowne, Inc.; *top right* courtesy of Sub-Zero; *bottom* courtesy of LG **page 65:** *left* courtesy of Sub-Zero; *right* courtesy of Thermador **page 66:** *top* Mark Lohman; *bottom* davidduncanlivingston.com **page 67:** *top* courtesy of U-Line; *bottom* courtesy of Sub-Zero **page 68:** courtesy of Sub-Zero **page 69:** *top* courtesy of Wolf; *bottom* courtesy of Sub-Zero **page 70:** *all* Merle Henkenius **page 71:** *left* courtesy of GE; *top right* courtesy of Whirlpool; *bottom right* courtesy of Miele **page 72–75:** *all* Merle Henkenius **page 76–79:** *all* Freeze Frame Studio/CH **page 80:** *top left* Olson Photographic, LLC, design: Jack Rosen Custom Kitchens; *top right* courtesy of Merillat; *bottom both* Mark Lohman, *(right)* design: Barclay Butera Inc. **page 81:** *top* Mark Lohman; *bottom both* Olson Photographic, LLC, *right* design: InnerSpace Electronics, *left* architect: Karin Patriquin **page 82–85:** *all* Freeze Frame Studio/CH **page 86:** *top* courtesy of Moen; *bottom* courtesy of Kohler **page 87:** *top* Rob Melnychuk; *bottom both* courtesy of Kohler **page 88–89:** Freeze Frame Studio/CH; *bottom right* courtesy of Kohler **page 90–91:** *all* Freeze Frame Studio/CH **page 92:** *all* courtesy of Kraftmaid **page 110:** John Parsekian/CH

Metric Conversion

Length

1 inch	25.4 mm
1 foot	0.3048 m
1 yard	0.9144 m
1 mile	1.61 km

Area

1 square inch	645 mm²
1 square foot	0.0929 m²
1 square yard	0.8361 m²
1 acre	4046.86 m²
1 square mile	2.59 km²

Volume

1 cubic inch	16.3870 cm³
1 cubic foot	0.03 m³
1 cubic yard	0.77 m³

Common Lumber Equivalents

Sizes: Metric cross sections are so close to their U.S. sizes, as noted below, that for most purposes they may be considered equivalents.

Dimensional lumber	1 x 2	19 x 38 mm
	1 x 4	19 x 89 mm
	2 x 2	38 x 38 mm
	2 x 4	38 x 89 mm
	2 x 6	38 x 140 mm
	2 x 8	38 x 184 mm
	2 x 10	38 x 235 mm
	2 x 12	38 x 286 mm
Sheet sizes	4 x 8 ft.	1200 x 2400 mm
	4 x 10 ft.	1200 x 3000 mm
Sheet thicknesses	¼ in.	6 mm
	⅜ in.	9 mm
	½ in.	12 mm
	¾ in.	19 mm
Stud/joist spacing	16 in. o.c.	400 mm o.c.
	24 in. o.c.	600 mm o.c.

Capacity

1 fluid ounce	29.57 mL
1 pint	473.18 mL
1 quart	1.14 L
1 gallon	3.79 L

Weight

1 ounce	28.35g
1 pound	0.45kg

Temperature

Celsius = Fahrenheit – 32 x ⅝

Fahrenheit = Celsius x 1.8 + 32

Nail Size (Penny) and Length

Penny Size	Nail Length
2d	1"
3d	1¼"
4d	1½"
5d	1¾"
6d	2"
7d	2¼"
8d	2½"
9d	2¾"
10d	3"
12d	3¼"
16d	3½"